50 Nifty Quilled Cards

50 Nifty Quilled Cards

Alli Bartkowski

LARK BOOKS

A Division of Sterling Publishing Co., Inc.
New York / London

SENIOR EDITOR
Terry Taylor

EDITOR
Linda Kopp

ART DIRECTOR
Kathy Holmes

ASSOCIATE ART DIRECTOR
Shannon Yokeley

PHOTOGRAPHER
John Widman

COVER DESIGNER
Cindy LaBreacht

Library of Congress Cataloging-in-Publication Data

Bartkowski, Alli.
  50 nifty quilled cards / Alli Bartkowski. -- 1st ed.
      p. cm.
  Includes index.
  ISBN-13: 978-1-60059-233-1 (pb-trade pbk. : alk. paper)
  ISBN-10: 1-60059-233-3 (pb-trade pbk. : alk. paper)
  1. Paper quillwork. 2. Greeting cards. I. Title. II. Title: Fifty nifty quilled cards.
TT870.B24193 2008
745.54--dc22

                                        2007046971

10 9 8 7 6 5 4 3 2 1

First Edition

Published by Lark Books, A Division of
Sterling Publishing Co., Inc.
387 Park Avenue South, New York, NY 10016

Text © 2008, Alli Bartkowski
Photography © 2008, Lark Books unless otherwise specified
Illustrations © 2008, Alli Bartkowski

Distributed in Canada by Sterling Publishing,
c/o Canadian Manda Group, 165 Dufferin Street
Toronto, Ontario, Canada M6K 3H6

Distributed in the United Kingdom by GMC Distribution Services,
Castle Place, 166 High Street, Lewes, East Sussex, England BN7 1XU

Distributed in Australia by Capricorn Link (Australia) Pty Ltd.,
P.O. Box 704, Windsor, NSW 2756 Australia

The written instructions, photographs, designs, patterns, and projects in this volume are intended for the personal use of the reader and may be reproduced for that purpose only. Any other use, especially commercial use, is forbidden under law without written permission of the copyright holder.

Every effort has been made to ensure that all the information in this book is accurate. However, due to differing conditions, tools, and individual skills, the publisher cannot be responsible for any injuries, losses, and other damages that may result from the use of the information in this book.

If you have questions or comments about this book, please contact:
Lark Books
67 Broadway
Asheville, NC 28801
828-253-0467

Manufactured in China

ISBN 13: 978-1-60059-233-1

For information about custom editions, special sales, premium and corporate purchases, please contact Sterling Special Sales Department at 800-805-5489 or specialsales@sterlingpub.com.

Contents

Introduction

Is someone you know celebrating a special occasion? Would you like to send a heartfelt as well as hand-crafted message? In just a few steps, you can create cards that are dimensional, eye-catching, and downright "wow" using delicate quilled paper forms.

Quilling is a fabulous way to embellish hand-made or store-bought cards. Making quilled shapes and scrolls is easy—simply roll a thin strip of paper into a coil and pinch it into your desired shape—but the results are impressive. The first time I saw a quilled frame decorated with delicate flowers and leaves, the coiled forms looked complicated. But when I rolled my first paper strip into a teardrop shape, I was thrilled by how effortless the process was. I soon started adding quilled shapes to all my cards, which served as great conversation starters at birthday parties and gave me the chance to share this rewarding paper art with others.

With just a little practice and a few tools, your cards can also become the talk of the party. In the Basics section, you'll learn about the tools and materials you need to get started, and how to create quilled shapes and scrolls. From there you'll be off and running with plenty of beauti-ful quilled cards to pick from. Choose an elegant design such as Cherish (page 30) or a whimsical project like Ice Cream Invite (page 38). Once you've mastered the basic shapes, you'll be ready for more challenging techniques like making alphabet letters using curled scrolls as seen in Monogram Glam, on page 118. Customizing the projects to fit your needs is a cinch by adding your own quote or greeting. Many of the cards have variations for even more design ideas and inspiration.

With over 50 design ideas in this book, you can make a quilled card for every occasion. Your creation will brighten a friend's day. (And no one ever has to know how easy it was for you to make.)

Basics

CARD BASICS

Based on the simple yet stunning creation of wound paper coils, quilling is a great way to add texture, dimension, and fun to your handmade cards. With just a few materials, tools, and simple techniques, you can make any one of the wonderful quilled cards in this book, or use the techniques and designs as inspiration for your own creations. You'll find cards that are perfect for a specific holiday or occasion, or anytime you want to make someone feel extra special.

Materials

If you love paper crafting, most of these materials and supplies are already in your crafting toolbox.

Paper

Cardstock comes is a variety of colors, textures, and weights. While solid colors are often used as the card base, it's nice to have a variety of shades and coordinating colors for layering. For even more variation, try printed cardstock, white cardstock that has a color printed on both sides. When the edges are sanded, you get a nice, worn look.

If you need something a little fancier, there is an amazing variety of printed papers that range in color, pattern, and texture. You can also experiment with vellums, translucent paper with a texture or print design. It's best to adhere this type of paper with brads or adhesive tabs, positioned so they won't be visible on the card front.

Embellishments

Embellishments are a fun way to add even more color and excitement to your quilled cards. For a textural design option, try adding ribbon to your cards in a variety of ways using ties, wraps, or knots. Available in an array of shapes, colors, and sizes, brads are metal fasteners that can be decorative as well as useful.

Many embellishments, such as beads, buttons, and rhinestones, have adhesive backs to make them fast and easy to apply. They can be found with the scrapbooking accessories in your craft store. But you don't have to go to the store to get great trimmings; search your craft supplies for one-of-a-kind embellishment ideas.

Tools

Once you've gathered the proper materials, make sure you've got these card-making tools on hand.

Cutting Tools

Craft stores are stocked full of tools for precision and decorative cutting jobs, but there are a few you won't want to go without. First and foremost, you'll need a sharp cutting knife and a cutting mat, to protect your work surface. If you find yourself cutting a lot of long, straight edges—as you most likely will in card-making

and quilling—consider investing in a 12-inch (30.5 cm) paper cutter, perfect for cardstock and quilling strips. Most trimmers also have a scoring blade for making folds in cardstock.

A hole punch is used to create a hole in cardstock, enabling you to add a ribbon. Besides the classic hole punch, paper punches are available in a variety of decorative shapes such as leaves and hearts. You can add interest to plain, straight edges with deckle, zigzag, or scallop-edged scissors, and a crimper is great for making wave or corrugated patterns in your paper. If you'd like to create a worn look on your card edges, sand the edges with sandpaper or a nail file.

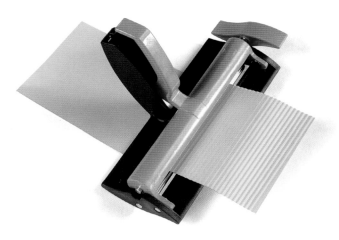

Art Supplies

Head to the art supply section of your craft store for plenty of card embellishing ideas. Chalk and watercolor paints are perfect when you need a hint of color, while ink pens, ink pads, and stamps can help you create those priceless, handmade details.

Note: Use your stamping supplies to create a worn or faded look for your card; just rub the ink pad along your cardstock edge.

Adhesives

For cards, follow these simple guidelines: use adhesive tabs when you need a sticky surface on both sides; foam squares where you want to add dimension; glue dots to attach ribbon and vellum; and for sparkle anytime, grab some glitter glue. For an authentic homemade look, skip the glue and sew on embellishments with a needle and thread or, if you're in a hurry, a sewing machine.

Techniques

With just a few folds, cards are quite easy to make. For a traditional look that's simple, try the basic folded card. Simply score a line down the middle of a cardstock sheet, and then fold the sheet in half along the line.

For something a little more involved, fashion a tri-fold card. This type of card is made with two scoring lines that create side panels that fold inward like a gate. A window card, a basic folded card with an opening—or window—cut in the card front, makes a dramatic presentation.

Tip: Try using a commercially printed card. Preprinted cards will save you time, and they usually come with a coordinating envelope. Simply add your personal touch to the pattern on the front with quilling and other embellishments.

QUILLING BASICS

One of the best things about quilled cards is that it only takes a few materials and tools to craft stunning one-of-a-kind creations. Before you get started, you'll need a few standard quilling materials, tools, and techniques.

Materials

The only special materials you'll need for quilling are paper strips.

Paper Strips

Precision-cut quilling paper strips come in a number of different lengths, widths, and weights. For quilled cards, the narrow widths, such as $\frac{1}{16}$ inch (1.6 mm) or ⅛ inch (3 mm), work best. Use the wider widths—¼ inch (6 mm) or ⅜ inch (9.5 mm)— for fringing flowers (page 15).

You can also cut your own paper strips with a paper cutter. As a general guide, most quilling is done with text-weight paper, because it's easier to roll and allows for highly intricate shapes. Thicker cardstock strips may be more difficult to roll, but they're perfect if your card calls for big and bold quilled shapes.

Tools

Along with your card-making tools, you'll need these specialized quilling tools, designed to help you quickly roll your paper strips. These tools are inexpensive and can be found in your craft store or online quilling store.

Basic Quilling Toolbox
Slotted tool
Needle tool
Fine-tipped tweezers
Toothpicks
Scissors
Ruler or circle sizer ruler
Straight pins
Corkboard or foam board
Craft glue

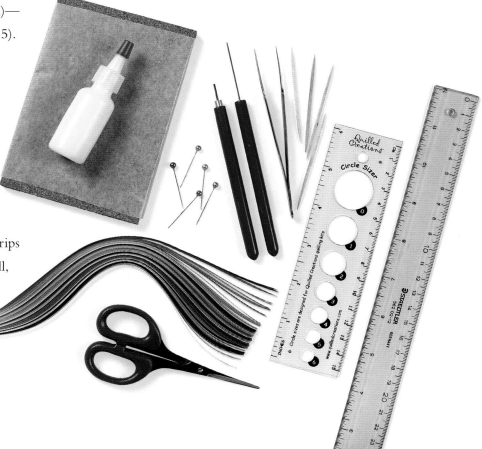

10

Circle sizer—This plastic template (see photo on opposite page) is useful for creating same-sized coils (such as snowflakes or flower petals) and off-center circles. Rolled paper is placed in a hole cutout and allowed to expand to that size. The paper end is then glued to maintain the coil size.

Slotted tool—Perfect for beginners, the slotted tool holds the paper's end so that you can immediately start rolling the paper by spinning the tool.

Toothpick—Simple but necessary, a toothpick is used to apply glue to the end of a strip after rolling. It also can be used for rolling, like the needle tool.

Needle tool—Basically a tapered needle set into a handle, the needle tool takes a little more practice but most quillers prefer this tool because of the smaller center. The needle tool can also be used for scoring, paper piercing, and placing glue in small amounts on the paper strips.

Straight pins—Straight pins are great for holding your quilled shapes together on a corkboard and for the off-center circle technique (see page 16).

Cork or foam board—The cork or foam board surface is used for the off-center circle technique, and, when it is covered with wax paper, the glued pieces will not stick to your work surface.

Fine-tip tweezers—Tweezers are essential for working with small quilled pieces. It's the perfect tool for gluing quilled shapes onto a card.

Craft glue—In quilling, you only need small dabs of glue to hold your coils together since you are gluing paper to paper. Choose a liquid or water-based glue that dries clear. Avoid overly tacky glues that are hard to remove from your fingers and tools; these can slow you down and ruin the quilled shapes.

Fine-tip scissors—Scissors with a fine-tip are used for hand fringing, trimming, and cutting detailed shapes.

Ruler—A ruler is helpful for measuring your cardstock and paper strips to size.

Techniques

Quilling is based on simple paper coils, but it's a little more involved than that. With a few adjustments, the basic rolling technique can be used to create a variety of quilled shapes for your cards. Whether you're using a slotted tool, a needle tool, a toothpick, or no tool at all, once you've mastered the basic paper rolling method, the rest is easy.

Rolling with a Slotted Tool

1 Insert the end of the paper strip into the slot from the top.

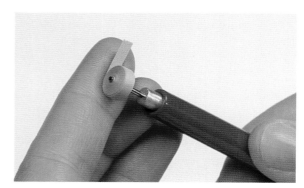

2 Begin rolling the paper strip around the tip by rotating the tool in either direction.

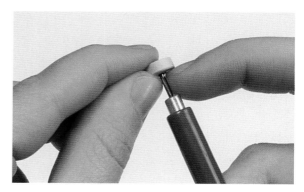

3 To keep the coil's center from being pulled out, remove the coil by pushing from behind or underneath the coil instead of pulling it off.

Using a Needle Tool or Toothpick

1 Scratch the end of the paper with your nail to soften the paper fibers. This will make it easier to wrap the paper end around the needle tip. You can also moisten the end of the paper strip slightly so that it sticks to the needle when you are ready to roll it.

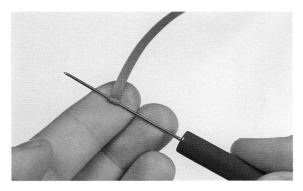

2 To start the roll, squeeze the end of the paper around the needle and roll it between your fingers without rotating the needle tool. The roll will start forming once the paper end is tucked under itself.

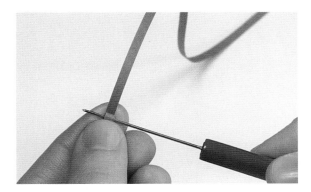

3 Continue to use light pressure, rolling the paper around the needle tool by moving your thumb and finger in opposite directions.

4 Slide the coil off the needle tool.

Finger Rolling

1 Scratch the end of the paper with your nail to soften the paper fibers.

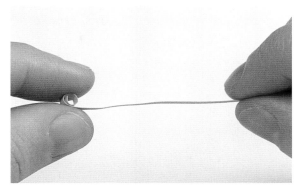

2 Gently press and curl the paper end between your thumb and finger so that the center of the coil forms.

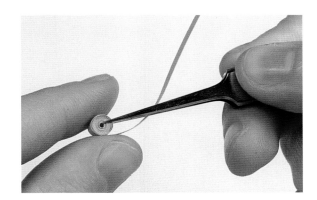

3 Start rolling the paper between your fingers. Use fine-tipped tweezers to help hold edges of the coil while rolling.

13

> **TIP**
>
> *Tear quilling strips to the specified length instead of cutting. The torn feathered end leaves a less obvious seam after gluing.*

Attaching End-to-End

Overlap the ends of two paper strips and glue them together. Roll the paper strip.

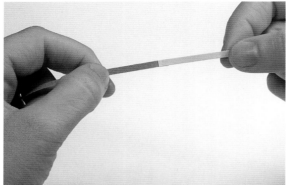

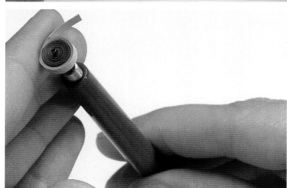

Rolling Multiple Strips

For added color and dimension, stack and glue two paper strips together. Then roll both of them at the same time using a tool or your fingers.

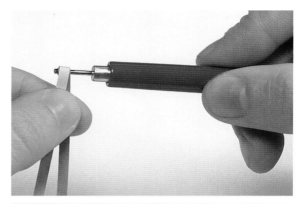

Fringing

For this technique, you'll need two widths of paper strips: ¼-inch (6 mm) (or wider) and ⅛ inch (3 mm).

1 To begin, fold the ¼-inch (6 mm) paper in half lengthwise. Starting at the fold, cut slits into the paper.

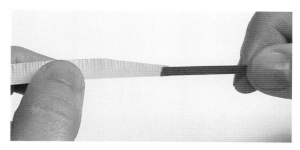

2 Unfold the paper strip and trim the fringes at an angle. Glue a strip of ⅛-inch-wide (3 mm) paper to the end of the fringed paper strip.

3 Start rolling from the ⅛-inch-wide (3 mm) paper end. Glue the end to the roll like a tight circle and fluff the fringes outward.

Adhering Quilled Shapes to a Card

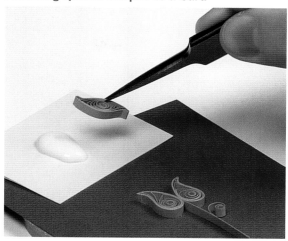

It's easy to attach quilled pieces to a card. All you need are glue, tweezers, and a steady hand.

1 Create a puddle of glue on a small notepad.

2 Using tweezers, pick up your quilled piece and place it in the glue.

3 Gently tap off the excess glue, and position the quilled shape on your card.

Signed and Delivered

Before you smack a stamp on your precious creation and stick it in the mailbox, take a moment to consider your mailing options. With just a few precautions and the proper packaging, you can make sure your fabulous quilled shapes arrive intact. First, try wrapping the card in bubble wrap or using a CD mailer box, perfect for most card sizes. Then do a little research at your local post office, paying careful attention to postal size and shape requirements. You may have to pay a little extra to ship your greeting or spend some extra time packing it, but your recipient's reaction will be well worth it.

Basic Quilled Shapes

Many of these basic shapes start with either a tight or a loose circle, but the results are quite different. See the sidebar on the facing page for shaping techniques.

TIGHT CIRCLE

To create a tight circle, roll the strip of paper until you've reached the end. Glue the end to the roll, not letting the coil expand open.

LOOSE CIRCLE

For a loose circle, start by rolling a paper strip as you did with the tight circle. Remove the coil from the tool and let it spring open. Place a small dab of glue on the loose end, and press it against the coil.

TIGHT OVAL OR MARQUISE

Roll a long strip of paper as you did with the tight circle, but do not glue the end to the roll yet. Gently allow the coil to expand a small amount, and glue the end to the roll. Pinch the desired shape.

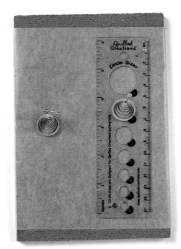

OFF-CENTER CIRCLE

Place a loose circle on a cork board or in a circle sizer, and pin the center of the coil to one side. Spread a thin layer of glue over the paper edges between the pins, and let it dry.

16

MARQUISE

Starting with a loose circle, use both hands to pinch points at opposite sides of the circle at the same time.

LOOSE CIRCLE WITH TAIL

Start by rolling a loose circle but leave a small section of the paper end straight. Glue the coil to the straightened end. From here, you have the option to leave your shape as a circle or pinch it into a teardrop.

TEARDROP

The teardrop is easier than it looks. Roll a loose circle and simply pinch a point on the coil.

SQUARE OR DIAMOND

Using a loose circle as your base, make a marquise. Turn it 90° and, making sure each side is roughly the same length, pinch two more points on opposite sides.

You can make just about any shape using loose circles by simply pinching a point or points.

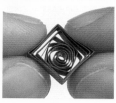

Curving points on a quilled shape gives you even more shaping options. Curl the points of any quilled shape—for example, the marquise—with your fingers or against the tip of the quilling tool for added flair. Pinch the point or points next to the glued paper end to hide the seam.

To help you size and arrange your shapes correctly, many card projects include templates, beginning on page 120.

HALF CIRCLE

For the half circle, start with a teardrop. Pinch a second point near the first point. The distance between the two pinched points determines how tall the half circle will be.

17

TRIANGLE

Alter a loose circle to make a teardrop. Press the rounded end inward to form two additional points.

RECTANGLE

Using a loose circle as your base, make a marquise and turn it slightly. Pinch two more points on opposite sides, creating two short sides and two long sides.

Basic Quilled Scrolls

Because the ends are left unglued, quilled scrolls have a different look than quilled shapes but are perfect when your card needs a few elegant curves.

LOOSE SCROLL
The loose scroll is quite simple. Start rolling the paper at one end, leaving the other end loose or straight.

HEART SCROLL
Make a fold at the center of the strip of paper. Roll each end inward toward the fold.

"S" SCROLL
Roll one paper end to the middle of the paper strip. Turn the strip around, and roll the other end toward the middle.

"Y" SCROLL
Make a fold at the center of the paper strip and roll each end outward. Place a small amount of glue on the inside of the fold and press together.

"C" SCROLL
Roll both ends of the paper toward the center.

"V" SCROLL
Make a fold at the center of the paper strip and roll each end outward.

SWOOPING SCROLL
First roll a "C," "S," or loose scroll, and then unravel part of the scroll. Gently re-roll the scroll, making the coils farther apart.

SCROLLED FLOWER
Measure and cut four strips of paper to the same length, and fold each in half to mark the middle. Glue the strips together in the middle in a wheel spoke pattern. Roll each paper end inward.

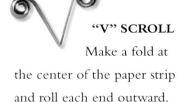

FOLDED LOOP
Make a fold at the center of the paper strip. Depending on the final shape, either glue at the fold or along the entire length of the paper, and press together. Shape the folded paper strip to the desired design.

A Card for Any Occasion

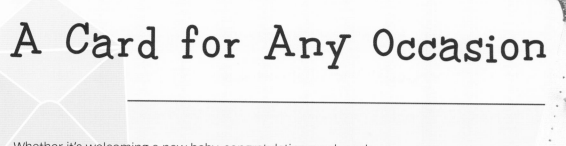

Whether it's welcoming a new baby, congratulating newlyweds, or celebrating a holiday, make your card stand out from the usual commercially made, store-bought cards. With just a touch of quilling, it's easy to make custom cards for any occasion.

Sweet Treat

Sweet tooths beware—you'll have to do your best to resist this delectable cupcake creation topped with tempting quilled frosting and a cherry.

FINISHED SIZE: 4 x 5 inches (10.2 x 12.7 cm)

MATERIALS

- Template (page 124)
- Cardstock: yellow and light blue
- Preprinted card
- Quilling paper: brown and red
- Brown ink pad
- Crimper tool
- Adhesive foam squares
- Brads

QUILLING SHAPES & SCROLLS
(pages 16–18)

- "C" scroll
- Loose circle with a tail

■ STEP BY STEP

1 Cut a circle from yellow cardstock, color the edges with brown ink, and adhere it to the front of a preprinted card.

2 For the cupcake frosting, roll five 4-inch (10.2 cm) lengths of brown quilling paper into "C" scrolls.

3 For the cherry, roll a 4-inch (10.2 cm) strip of red quilling paper into a loose circle with a tail.

4 For the wrapper, cut a 2-inch-square (5 cm) piece from light blue cardstock. Run the piece through the crimper, and trim it into a trapezoid shape. Adhere the cupcake wrapper to the yellow circle with foam squares, leaving space for the quilled shapes.

5 Glue the quilled pieces in place on the card front. Insert brads into the side of the card for an extra touch of color.

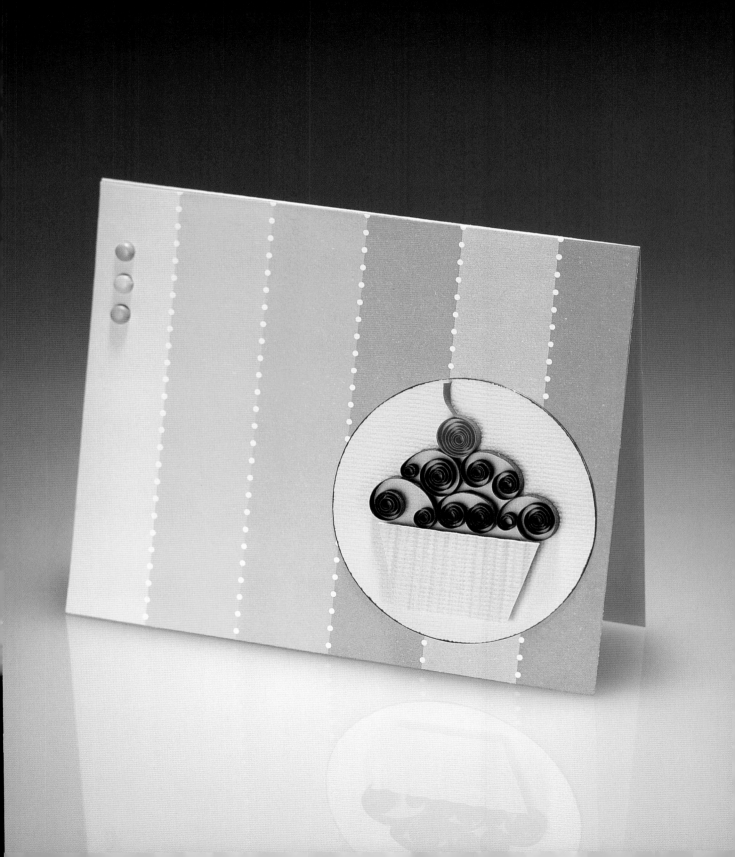

Hoppy Birthday

Complete with a lily pad, a buzzing fly, and a silly smile, this happy frog will brighten anyone's birthday. In a snap you can change the text to a different greeting, or use a different animal altogether.

FINISHED SIZE: 3¼ x 4¼ inches (8.3 x 10.8 cm)

MATERIALS

- Template (page 121)
- Cardstock: printed stripe pattern and light green
- Printed floral paper
- Quilling paper: green, red, and black
- Corner rounder punch
- Green chalk
- "Hoppy Birthday" text (computer generated)
- Glitter glue
- Black fine-tip pen
- Wiggly eyes

QUILLING SHAPES & SCROLLS

(pages 16–18)

- Tight oval
- Half circle
- Folded loop
- Off-center circle

■ STEP BY STEP

1 Fold a 6½ x 4¼-inch (16.5 x 10.8 cm) piece of printed stripe cardstock in half to make a basic folded card that measures 3¼ x 4¼ inches (8.3 x 10.8 cm). Round the corners of the card.

2 Cut a circle from the floral printed paper, and adhere it to the card front. Cut a lily pad shape from the light green cardstock, rub the edges with green chalk, and adhere it to the card.

3 Adhere the text to the card. Add glitter glue along the printed paper stripes and on the lily pad.

4 For the frog's head and face, glue multiple strips of green quilling paper end-to-end to make a 48-inch (121.9 cm) paper strip. Roll it into a tight oval. With a black pen, draw the nose and mouth. Glue two wiggly eyes to the face. For the tongue, cut and roll a small narrow length of red quilling paper, and glue it to the frog's mouth.

5 For the body, roll a 16-inch (40.6 cm) length of green quilling paper into an off-center circle. Then pinch the shape into a half circle.

Variation: If you prefer dogs to frogs, change the theme for an entirely different look.

hoppy birthday

6 For the back feet, roll two 4-inch (10.2 cm) pieces of green quilling paper into half circles. Make the legs by cutting two 2-inch (5 cm) strips of green and folding each one in half to create a folded loop. Glue the loops to the feet.

7 For the front feet, cut a 3-inch (7.6 cm) length of green quilling paper in half lengthwise to make a narrow 1/16-inch-wide (1.6 mm) paper strip. Roll each piece into a half circle.

8 For the fly, make small folds in strips of black quilling paper to create an "M" shape. Glue the ends together, and use tweezers to open the loops. Glue the fly to the card, and add the fly's trail with the black pen. Glue the rest of the pieces in place on the card front.

24

Mother's Day Bouquet

Surprise mom with a bouquet of quilled flowers. Fringing these flowers will be time well spent to show mom how much you appreciate her, and, best of all, these beautiful blooms will last forever.

FINISHED SIZE: 6 x 4 inches (15.2 x 10.2 cm)

MATERIALS

- Template (page 120)
- Cardstock: light plum and dark plum
- Printed pattern paper
- ⅛-inch (3 mm) quilling paper: ivory, moss green, and pink
- ¼-inch (6 mm) quilling paper: pink, fuchsia, and raspberry
- Green tissue paper
- Green ribbon
- Glue dots

■ STEP BY STEP

1 Fold a 6 x 8-inch (15.2 x 20.3 cm) piece of dark plum cardstock twice to create a 6 x 4-inch (15.2 x 10.2 cm) tri-fold card.

2 Cut a piece of printed paper that is slightly smaller than the card front. Cut the piece in half and adhere one half to each side panel.

3 Cut a 3 x 2-inch (7.6 x 5 cm) oval from the dark plum cardstock. Adhere it to light plum cardstock and trim around the oval, leaving a small light plum border. Using the photo as a guide, adhere the oval to the left panel on the card front.

4 Cut a 2 x 2-inch (5 x 5 cm) square from the green tissue paper; fold it into a diamond shape, as shown in the template, and adhere it to the oval. Tie a ribbon into a bow and attach it

on top of the green tissue paper with glue dots.

5 For the flowers, use the ¼-inch (6 mm) quilling paper, and fringe a 2-inch (5 cm) length following the fringing technique (page 15).

6 Attach a 2-inch (5 cm) length of the skinnier quilling paper to the fringe end using the end-to-end technique (page 14), and, starting from the skinnier strip, roll the strip into a flower.

7 Glue the roll into a tight circle, and gently fluff the fringes outward. Repeat steps 5 through 7 to make six fringed flowers. Place the quilled shapes on the card front, and glue them in place.

TIP

To save time with the fringing technique, fold a ¼-inch-wide (6 mm) paper strip in half, and fringe two layers at once.

Set Sail

With torn paper waves and tiny quilled gulls, you can almost smell the salt air. A quilled sailboat riding atop of "S" scroll waves completes this peaceful ocean scene.

FINISHED SIZE: 5 x 4 inches (12.7 x 10.2 cm)

MATERIALS

- Template (page 124)
- Cardstock: orange, yellow, and blue
- Blue printed paper
- Quilling paper: light blue, white, black, and light brown
- Chalk: red and orange

QUILLING SHAPES & SCROLLS

(pages 16–18)

- Triangle
- Marquise
- "S" scroll

■ STEP BY STEP

1 Create a basic folded 5 x 4-inch (12.7 x 10.2 cm) card using a 10 x 4-inch (25.4 x 10.2 cm) piece of orange cardstock.

2 Cut a 2-inch-diameter (5 cm) circle from yellow cardstock for the sun. Rub the edge with orange and red chalk.

3 Cut a rectangle from blue cardstock and printed blue paper. Tear one side and bend the torn edges down to create waves.

4 Before adhering the paper pieces to the card front, lay the sun and wave pieces out on the card. Rub red chalk along the water horizon to create the sunset, and adhere the sun and wave pieces to the card.

5 For the sails, roll two 16-inch (40.6 cm) pieces of white quilling paper into right-angle triangles, making one triangle taller than the other. For the mast, fold a 3-inch (7.6 cm) length of black quilling paper, using the template as a guide.

6 Roll a 16-inch (40.6 cm) length of light brown quilling paper into a marquise to make the boat. Pinch a third point to create the back of the boat.

7 For the waves, roll three 4-inch (10.2 cm) lengths of light blue quilling paper into "S" scrolls.

8 Create the seagulls by cutting a ½-inch (1.3 cm) piece of white quilling paper in half lengthwise to create two narrow paper strips. Use tweezers to fold and bend the paper strips into seagulls. Glue the quilled shapes in place on the card.

Two Peas in a Pod

Twins, best friends, sisters, or brothers—share this card with someone very close to you. Embellish with ribbons and buttons for a one-of-a-kind look.

FINISHED SIZE: 5¼ x 4 inches (13.3 x 10.2 cm)

MATERIALS
- Template (page 123)
- Cardstock: dark green, light green, and ivory
- Printed green gingham paper
- Quilling paper: moss green
- Ribbons
- Buttons
- Zigzag scissors

QUILLING SHAPES & SCROLLS
(pages 16–18)
- Loose circle
- Folded loop

■ STEP BY STEP

1 Fold an 5¼ x 8¼-inch (13.3 x 21 cm) piece of dark green cardstock twice to create a 5¼ x 4-inch (13.3 x 10.2 cm) tri-fold card.

2 Cut a piece of gingham paper so it's slightly smaller than one of the panels, and adhere it to the front panel.

3 Cut a 1½ x 1¾-inch (3.8 x 4.4 cm) rectangle from ivory cardstock. Adhere it to light green cardstock, and trim the edges with zigzag scissors, leaving a green border showing.

4 Cut three pieces of ribbon, and glue them to the small rectangular piece. Adhere the ribbon and cardstock pieces to the top panel on the card front.

5 Glue the buttons to the bottom left corner of the card.

6 Roll two 8-inch (20.3 cm) lengths of moss-green quilling paper into loose circles to make the peas. For the pod, use an 8-inch (20.3 cm) piece of moss green. Fold the strip in half twice, and glue it into a pod shape. Glue the pieces in place on the card front.

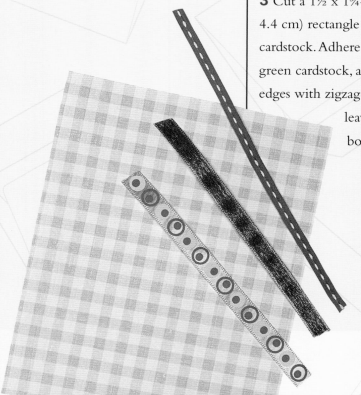

Cherish

With heart-shaped accents and graceful swooping scrolls, this card is pure romance, a perfect way to show your affection.

FINISHED SIZE: 5 x 4 inches (12.7 x 10.2 cm)

MATERIALS

- Template (page 124)
- Cardstock: light purple and dark purple
- Vellum with ivory floral print
- Quilling paper: ivory
- Pewter heart brads
- "Cherish" metal charm

QUILLING SHAPES & SCROLLS

(page 18)

- Heart scroll
- Swooping scroll

■ STEP BY STEP

1 Create a basic folded 5 x 4-inch (12.7 x 10.2 cm) card using a 5 x 8-inch (12.7 x 20.3 cm) piece of light purple cardstock.

2 Cut a 5 x 3-inch (12.7 x 7.6 cm) rectangle from vellum. Cut a smaller rectangle from dark purple cardstock, and adhere both pieces to the card front.

3 Insert the heart brads, and attach the metal charm to the card.

4 Use three 2-inch (5 cm) and three 4-inch (10.2 cm) pieces of ivory quilling paper to roll swooping scrolls.

5 For the heart, roll a 2-inch (5 cm) length of ivory quilling paper into a heart scroll. Attach the quilled shapes to the card front.

31

Variation: *For a formal look, try a black and ivory color scheme.*

Plum Vines

A modern floral border is easy to craft with basic quilled shapes and scrolls. Zigzag stitching adds even more texture to this contemporary greeting.

FINISHED SIZE: 4 x 5 inches (10.2 x 12.7 cm)

MATERIALS
- Template (page 122)
- Cardstock: white and pink
- Floral-printed paper
- Cardstock quilling strips: plum and light green
- Sewing machine

QUILLING SHAPES & SCROLLS
(pages 16–18)
- Teardrop
- Marquise
- "S" scroll

32

■ STEP BY STEP

1 Fold an 8 x 5-inch (20.3 x 12.7 cm) piece of white cardstock in half to create a 4 x 5-inch (10.2 x 12.7 cm) card.

2 Cut a piece of floral-printed paper so it's slightly smaller than the card front, and adhere it to the card.

3 Cut a 1½ x 5-inch (3.8 x 12.7 cm) strip of pink cardstock, adhere it to the card front, and zigzag stitch along each edge, using a sewing machine.

4 Using plum cardstock quilling strips, create the flowers by rolling one 6-inch (15.2 cm) strip and two 4-inch (10.2 cm) strips into marquise shapes. Glue together with the larger marquise in the center.

5 For the flower buds, roll two 4-inch (10.2 cm) lengths of plum cardstock quilling strips into teardrops.

6 For the scrolls, roll two 4-inch (10.2 cm) strips of light green cardstock quilling paper into swooping "S" scrolls.

7 For the leaves, roll two 4-inch (10.2 cm) lengths of light green cardstock quilling strips into marquise shapes. Place the quilled shapes on the card front, and glue them in place.

Holiday Holly

The holly is a favorite holiday icon. Use punched leaves and roll loose circles to create perfect accents for your holiday greetings.

FINISHED SIZE: 2½ x 4 inches (6.4 x 10.2 cm)

MATERIALS
- Cardstock: crimson and moss green
- Green striped printed paper
- Quilling paper: crimson
- Embroidery needle
- Green embroidery thread
- Hole punch
- Red ribbon
- Leaf paper punch

QUILLING SHAPES & SCROLLS
(pages 16–17)
- Loose circle

■ STEP BY STEP

1 Create a basic 2½ x 4-inch (6.4 x 10.2 cm) tag from the crimson cardstock.

2 Cut a piece of green printed paper slightly smaller than the tag, and adhere it to the front.

3 Using the embroidery needle (or quilling needle tool), measure and pierce evenly spaced holes on the top and bottom of the tag along the edge of the printed paper. Make a zigzag stitch using green thread.

4 Punch a hole and attach a ribbon at the top of the tag.

5 Punch two leaves from the moss green cardstock, and adhere them to the tag.

6 For the holly berries, roll three 2-inch (5 cm) lengths of crimson quilling paper into loose circles. Determine the placement of the quilled pieces, and glue each piece in place.

Variation: Make a whole quilled wreath for added holiday cheer.

Butterfly in Flight

Flitting from one sun-drenched flower to the next, the butterfly is the embodiment of a free spirit. Recreate its graceful flight using both stamped and quilled images.

FINISHED SIZE: 4 x 5 inches (10.2 x 12.7 cm)

MATERIALS & TOOLS

- Template (page 123)
- Cardstock: light yellow and yellow
- Quilling paper: deep yellow and white
- Light brown ink pad
- Butterfly stamp
- Striped ribbon

QUILLING SHAPES & SCROLLS

(pages 16–18)

- Teardrop
- "Y" scroll

■ STEP BY STEP

1 Fold a 4 x 10-inch (10.2 x 25.4 cm) piece of light yellow cardstock in half to make a 4 x 5-inch (10.2 x 12.7 cm) card, and rub the edges with light brown ink.

2 Cut a rectangular piece of yellow cardstock that is slightly smaller than the card front. Ink the edges with light brown, and adhere it to the card.

3 Use light brown ink to stamp butterflies in an arch pattern across the front of the card.

4 Tie a ribbon around the left edge of the card front.

5 For the quilled butterfly, roll four 8-inch (20.3 cm) lengths of yellow quilling strips into teardrops, making the size of the teardrops slightly larger than the butterfly stamp. Create the butterfly's body by rolling a "Y" scroll with white quilling paper. Place the quilled shapes on the card front, and glue them in place.

Variation: Experiment with different embellishments— such as flower-shaped brads or silk flowers—for a variety of fun results.

37

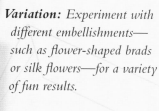

Ice Cream Invite

The hardest part about making quilled ice cream is picking the flavors. This yummy card can be used to announce a birthday party or an ice cream social.

FINISHED SIZE: 4 inches (10.2 cm) in diameter

MATERIALS

- Template (page 123)
- Preprinted polka-dot card
- Cardstock: light green and light blue
- Quilling paper: gold, red, light blue, pink, ivory, and mint green (or your favorite flavor)
- Text stamp or pen
- Hole punch
- Ribbon

QUILLING SHAPES & SCROLLS

(pages 16–17)

- Loose circle with a tail
- Triangle
- Half circle

Variation: Vary the ice cream flavors to make your own unique combination.

■ STEP BY STEP

1 Cut a preprinted polka-dot card into a circle that is 4 inches (10.2 cm) in diameter, making sure the fold is at the left side of the card.

2 Cut two strips of cardstock, one in light blue and a slightly wider one in light green. Glue the light blue piece on top of the light green piece, and adhere them to the card. Trim the ends following the curve of the card front.

3 Stamp or write "You're Invited" on a small strip of light green cardstock, adhere the strip to the card front, and trim the ends, again following the curve of the card front.

4 Punch three holes along the fold, and attach three ribbons.

5 For the ice cream cone, roll an 8-inch (20.3 cm) length of gold quilling paper into a triangle.

6 Roll 8-inch (20.3 cm) strips of quilling paper into half circles, and curve the points (page 17) to create the ice cream scoops.

7 For the cherry, roll a 1-inch (2.5 cm) piece of red quilling paper into a loose circle with a tail. Place the quilled shapes on the card front, and glue them in place.

Baby Bundle

This delightful quilled bow is a perfect topper for any gift package. Add a sweet charm to the front to make an extra special welcome for a newborn boy or girl.

FINISHED SIZE: 4 x 4 inches (10.2 x 10.2 cm)

MATERIALS

- Template (page 121)
- Cardstock: light green and white
- Light green gingham and striped printed paper
- Quilling paper: yellow
- Corner rounder punch or scissors
- Baby charm
- Light green ink pad

QUILLING SHAPES & SCROLLS

(pages 16–18)

- Tight circle
- Triangle
- Loose scroll

■ STEP BY STEP

1 Create a basic folded 4-inch (10.2 cm) square card from an 8 x 4-inch (20.3 x 10.2 cm) piece of light green cardstock. Round the edges of the card with a corner rounder punch or scissors.

2 Cut two long strip rectangles from printed paper and adhere them to the card front, using the photo as a guide.

3 Cut a small 1 x 2-inch (2.5 x 5 cm) tag from white cardstock, adhere it to the striped printed paper, and trim around the white cardstock to create a border.

4 Add a charm to the tag, and adhere the tag to the card front. Rub the edges of the card front with light green ink.

5 Create the bow by rolling two 8-inch (20.3 cm) lengths of yellow quilling paper strips into triangles. Roll an 8-inch (20.3 cm) strip of yellow quilling paper into a tight circle, and roll two 2-inch (5 cm) lengths into loose scrolls. Glue the quilled pieces in place on the card front.

Variation: Need a card for a girl? Use pink accents for an easy alteration.

Bluebell

Paisley swirls and a dramatic focal flower make this card one artful greeting. A color-coordinated ribbon adds additional texture and interest.

MATERIALS

- Template (page 123)
- Flower or paisley printed paper
- Cardstock: brown and moss green
- Quilling paper: light blue, yellow, and moss green
- Hole punch
- Ribbon

QUILLING SHAPES & SCROLLS

(pages 16–18)
- Loose circle with tail
- Marquise
- Triangle
- Loose scroll

■ STEP BY STEP

1 Create a basic folded 5 x 4-inch (12.7 x 10.2 cm) card using a 10 x 4-inch (25.4 x 10.2 cm) piece of printed paper.

2 Cut a 2½ x 3½ (6.4 x 8.9 cm) rectangle from the moss-green cardstock and a slightly smaller rectangle from the brown cardstock. Adhere the brown rectangle to the top of the moss-green cardstock.

3 Punch two holes at the top of the rectangles, and attach the ribbon. Adhere the rectangular pieces to the card front, using the photo as a guide.

4 Create the flower petals by rolling four 16-inch (40.6 cm) strips of light blue quilling paper into curved triangles.

5 Roll three 2-inch (5 cm) lengths of yellow quilling paper into loose circles with a tail to make the flower center.

6 For the leaves, roll two 16-inch (40.6 cm) pieces of moss-green quilling paper into marquise shapes. Roll a 4-inch (10.2 cm) length of moss-green quilling paper into a loose scroll for the stem. Place the quilled shapes on the card front, and glue them in place.

43

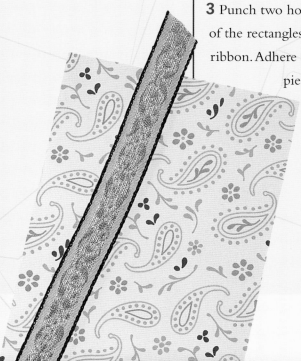

Easter Eggs Aplenty

*You'll have fun creating these cheerful eggs with quilled coils.
Vibrant colors make this card great for springtime, but you could
use a different window shape for another season or holiday.*

FINISHED SIZE: 3 x 3 inches (7.6 x 7.6 cm)

MATERIALS

- Template (page 120)
- Cardstock: yellow, dark yellow, and white
- Quilling paper: pink, light green, light blue, and lilac
- Yellow ink pad
- Craft knife
- Hole punch
- Chiffon ribbon: pink and green
- Foam adhesive squares

QUILLING SHAPES & SCROLLS

(pages 16–17)

- Loose circle

■ STEP BY STEP

1 Fold a piece of 3 x 6-inch (7.6 x 15.2 cm) dark yellow cardstock to create a square 3 x 3-inch (7.6 x 7.6 cm) card.

2 Cut a square piece of yellow cardstock slightly smaller than the card front. Rub the edges with yellow ink, and adhere the square to the card.

3 Cut a 1½ x 2-inch (3.8 x 5 cm) rectangle from white cardstock to make a tag, and rub the edges with yellow ink.

4 With the craft knife, trace and cut out the egg pattern to create a window. Punch a hole at the top, and attach a few strands of ribbon.

5 For the egg shapes, roll a variety of quilling paper strips—measuring from 2 to 8 inches (5 to 20.3 cm)—into loose circles.

6 Use tweezers to determine the placement of the quilled pieces on the card front, keeping in mind that the loose circles need to show through the window of the white tag. Glue each quilled coil in place.

7 Adhere the white tag to the card front with foam squares.

Variation: For a different look that's equally cute, use Easter eggs to create a tag like this one.

44

Cup of Kindness

Got a favorite friend for sharing good conversation and a hot cup of coffee? Add a whimsical saying—"Thanks a latte!" or "Coffee anyone?"—and send your pal this upbeat card.

FINISHED SIZE: 5 x 4 inches (12.7 x 10.2 cm)

MATERIALS

- Template (page 123)
- Cardstock: beige and dark brown
- Floral and striped printed papers
- Quilling paper: yellow and white
- Brown ink pad
- "Caffé?" text (computer generated or stamped)

QUILLING SHAPES & SCROLLS

(pages 16–18)

- Rectangle
- "S" scroll
- Loose scroll

■ STEP BY STEP

1 Create a 5 x 4-inch (12.7 x 10.2 cm) card by folding a 10 x 4-inch (25.4 x 10.2 cm) piece of beige cardstock in half. Ink the edges of the card with brown ink.

2 Cut a piece of striped printed paper that is a little bit smaller than the card front, ink the edges with brown ink, and adhere it to the card.

3 Cut a 1½ x 3½-inch (3.8 x 8.9 cm) rectangle from floral-printed paper, ink the edges, and adhere it to the card over the striped paper.

4 Using the brown cardstock, cut a circle that measures 1¼ inches (3.2 cm) in diameter, and adhere it to the card on top of the floral paper.

5 Print or write "Caffé?" on a piece of beige cardstock, and trim around the text to make an oval shape. Color the edges with brown ink, and adhere the oval to the card.

6 For the mug, roll a 16-inch (40.6 cm) length of yellow quilling paper into a rectangle. For the mug's handle, roll a 1-inch (2.5 cm) length of yellow quilling paper into an "S" scroll.

7 For the steam, roll strips of white quilling paper—measuring 1 to 2 inches (2.5 to 5 cm) in length—into loose scrolls and "S" scrolls. Position the quilled shapes on the card front, and glue them in place.

Love Doves

Create a romantic greeting for two lovebirds, whether young or old. A circular window in the vellum makes the smooching doves the focal point.

FINISHED SIZE: 8 x 3½ inches (20.3 x 8.9 cm)

MATERIALS

- Template (page 121)
- Cardstock: light gray and dark gray
- Vellum embossed floral paper
- Quilling paper: white and pink
- Glue dots
- Pearls
- Ribbon

QUILLING SHAPES & SCROLLS

(pages 16–17)
- Teardrop

■ STEP BY STEP

1 Create a rectangular 8 x 3½-inch (20.3 x 8.9 cm) card using an 8 x 7-inch (20.3 x 17.8 cm) piece of light gray cardstock. Cut a circle out of the card front.

2 Cut a piece of vellum that is slightly smaller than the card front, adhere it to the card front at the corners with glue dots, and create a circle cutout in the vellum that matches the position of the cutout on the card. Attach a pearl embellishment over each glue dot.

3 Cut a circle piece from dark gray cardstock, and adhere it to the inside of the card. Be sure that it is larger than the circle cutout on the card front.

4 Roll two 4-inch (10.2 cm) strips of pink quilling paper into teardrops, and glue them together to make the heart.

5 For the dove heads, roll two 4-inch (10.2 cm) pieces of white quilling paper into teardrops. For the dove bodies, roll two 12-inch (30.5 cm) pieces of white quilling paper into teardrops. Pinch a second point near the first point to create the dove's tail. Glue all the pieces in place on the card front.

6 Tie the ribbon around the card to keep it closed.

Merci Bouquet

No matter what country or in which language, nothing says "thank you" like a handmade card. Quilled centers and leaves paired with punched paper flowers make this card super quick to create.

FINISHED SIZE: 4 x 6 inches (10.2 x 15.2 cm)

MATERIALS

- Cardstock: orange, moss green, and dark green
- Floral-printed paper
- Cardstock quilling strips: dark green and yellow
- Black pen (or computer-generated text)
- Flower die cuts (optional)

QUILLING SHAPES & SCROLLS

(pages 16–17)

- Loose circle
- Marquise

■ STEP BY STEP

1 Fold an 8 x 6-inch (20.3 x 15.2 cm) piece of orange cardstock in half to create a 4 x 6-inch (10.2 x 15.2 cm) basic folded card. Cut a piece of floral-printed paper that's slightly smaller than the card, and adhere it to the front of the card.

2 Cut a 1¼ x 2¾-inch (3.2 x 7 cm) rectangle from dark green cardstock, and adhere it to the bottom right corner of the card.

3 Write or print "merci" on a moss-green strip of cardstock. Trim around the text, and adhere it on top of the dark green rectangle.

4 Cut out three flowers (or use die-cut flowers), and adhere them to the card front.

5 For the flower centers, roll three 6-inch (15.2 cm) yellow cardstock quilling strips into loose circles.

6 For the leaves, roll three 6-inch (15.2 cm) lengths of dark green cardstock quilling paper into marquise shapes, and then pinch to curve the points (page 17). Place the quilled shapes on the card front, and glue them in place.

Variation: Add some texture to your "Thank you" card with silk flower petals, rickrack, and a neat closure.

merci

Let It Snow

A chill is in the air! This endearing snowman is made of simple loose circles and decorated with a top hat and scarf. It's the perfect wintertime excuse to share a warm and friendly greeting.

FINISHED SIZE: 5 x 4 inches (12.7 x 10.2 cm)

MATERIALS

- Template (page 120)
- Cardstock: blue, dark blue, and white
- Snowflake-print paper
- Quilling paper: white, light green, and black
- White ribbon
- Stapler
- Snowflake punch

QUILLING SHAPES & SCROLLS
(pages 16–18)

- Loose circle
- Square
- Y scroll variation

■ STEP BY STEP

1 Fold a rectangular piece of 5 x 8-inch (12.7 x 20.3 cm) dark blue cardstock in half to create a 5 x 4-inch (12.7 x 10.2 cm) card.

2 Cut a piece of snowflake-printed paper slightly smaller than the card front, and adhere it to the card.

3 Cut one 2 x 3-inch (5 x 7.6 cm) rectangle from dark blue cardstock and one slightly smaller rectangle from blue cardstock. Glue the two pieces together, with the smaller rectangle on top. Staple a folded ribbon to the top of the rectangle pieces, and adhere the rectangle to the front of the card.

4 Make the snowman by rolling an 8-inch (20.3 cm) strip of white quilling paper into a loose circle for the head. For the body, roll a 12-inch (30.5 cm) length of white quilling paper into a loose circle.

5 For the hat, roll an 8-inch (20.3 cm) length of black quilling paper into a square. Roll the ends of a ½-inch (1.3 cm) strip of black paper, and glue it to the hat base for the brim.

6 To create the scarf, cut a 2-inch (5 cm) strip of light green quilling paper. Fold the strip in half, and roll the ends in the same direction. Place glue between the strips at the fold, and press together.

7 Using the photo as a guide, place the quilled shapes on the card front, and glue them in place. Punch out a single snowflake shape, and adhere it to the front of the card.

Variation: Use the same wintry theme to create a fun gift tag, perfect for a gift box or bag.

53

Bonbon Beauties

These chocolate sweets look good enough to eat! They're fast and easy to make with cardstock strips and zigzag scissors.

FINISHED SIZE: 4 x 5½ inches (10.2 x 14 cm)

MATERIALS

- Template (page 123)
- Cardstock: dark brown
- Candy-printed paper
- Cardstock quilling strips: light brown and dark brown
- Text paper: white and pink
- White ribbon
- Brads
- Zigzag scissors

QUILLING SHAPES & SCROLLS
(pages 16–17)

- Tight circle
- Square
- Triangle

■ STEP BY STEP

1 Create a basic folded 4 x 5½-inch (10.2 x 14 cm) card from an 8 x 5½-inch (20.3 x 14 cm) section of dark brown cardstock.

2 Cut a 2 x 5¼-inch (5 x 13.3 cm) rectangle piece from candy-printed paper, and adhere it to the top front of the card.

3 Adhere a white ribbon across the front of the card, and attach brads.

4 Create the bonbons using light and dark brown cardstock quilling strips. Cut two 12-inch (30.5 cm) lengths of dark brown quilling strips, and roll them into tight circles. Roll two 6-inch (15.2 cm) strips of light brown quilling paper into loose circles. Pinch one loose circle into a triangle and the other into a square.

5 For the wrappers, cut out two pink and two white circles with zigzag scissors. Glue the candy chocolates to the paper wrappers.

6 Make the decorative toppings on the chocolates by cutting thin strips of pink and white paper. Fold or roll different shapes, and glue them to the tops of the chocolates. Place the candies on the card front, and glue them in place.

Fourth of July Fireworks

Celebrate your patriotism with a bang. Cardstock quilling strips create bold and beautiful shapes that really "pop."

FINISHED SIZE: 4 x 5 inches (10.2 x 12.7 cm)

MATERIALS

- Template (page 120)
- Printed cardstock: red and blue
- Star printed paper
- Cardstock quilling strips: red, blue, white, and yellow
- Sandpaper
- Sewing machine
- Brown thread
- Star brads

QUILLING SHAPES & SCROLLS

(pages 16–18)

- Square
- Loose scroll
- Folded loop

■ STEP BY STEP

1 Fold an 8 x 5-inch (20.3 x 12.7 cm) piece of red printed cardstock in half to create a 4 x 5-inch (10.2 x 12.7 cm) card.

2 Cut a 4 x 4-inch (10.2 x 10.2 cm) piece of star paper and a 4 x 3½-inch (10.2 x 8.9 cm) piece from the printed blue cardstock. Tear the right edge of each piece, and adhere both pieces to the card front, using the photo as a guide. Sand the card edges.

3 Machine-stitch around the card front. Insert two star brads at the lower right corner.

4 For the firework, roll one 12-inch (30.5 cm) length of red, white, and blue cardstock quilling strips into a square, and glue the squares together. Cut a small length of white for the wick, and roll it into a loose scroll shape.

5 For the sparks, fold a 10-inch (25.4 cm) length of yellow cardstock quilling strip in half. Glue the strip together at the fold, and make a series of zigzag folds. Trim the spark to the desired length, glue the trimmed ends together, and shape the spark around the wick. Place all the quilled shapes on the card front, and glue them in place.

Variation: Use this card as inspiration for a cute gift tag, with stars, stripes, and plenty of patriotic fun.

Tulip Window Box

Imagine the smiles these dainty quilled tulips will bring! Your greeting will peek through this lovely window card, complete with a picket fence flower box.

FINISHED SIZE: 4 x 4 inches (10.2 x 10.2 cm)

MATERIALS
- Template (page 122)
- Cardstock: white and light green
- Quilling paper: green, pink, hot pink, purple, yellow, and raspberry
- Black pen
- Gray chalk
- Craft knife
- Foam adhesive squares

QUILLING SHAPES & SCROLLS
(pages 16–17)
- Marquise

 STEP BY STEP

1 Create a folded square 4-inch (10.2 cm) card using an 8 x 4-inch (20.3 x 10.2 cm) piece of white cardstock.

2 Cut a square piece from light green cardstock that is slightly smaller than 4 x 4 inches (10.2 x 10.2 cm), and adhere it to the inside of the card. Cut out four 1-inch (2.5 cm) squares from the card front to create a window effect.

3 For the picket fence, cut a ½ x 3-inch (1.3 x 7.6 cm) rectangle from white cardstock for a base. Cut eleven 1 x ¼-inch (2.5 x .6 cm) pieces for the pickets, and glue them evenly across the base. Trim the tops with scissors to create points, and draw in nail heads with a black pen.

4 Rub gray chalk around the card front and each fence piece.

5 Using the pink, hot pink, purple, yellow, and raspberry quilling strips, create each tulip by rolling two 8-inch (20.3 cm) lengths of quilling paper into marquise shapes and curve the points (page 17).

6 For the stem, use a 2- to 3-inch (5 to 7.6 cm) length of green quilling paper (depending on how tall you'd like your tulip to be), and fold it in half. Trim one end of the green strip into a narrow leaf, and glue the other end between the two tulip marquise shapes, using tweezers as needed. Place the quilled shapes on the card front, and glue them in place.

7 Place foam adhesive squares between the stems, and attach the fence piece.

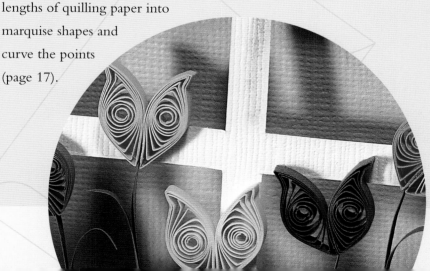

Little Ladybug

Framed by a cut-out window, this quilled ladybug is the picture of tranquility. She rests upon a hand-painted branch that's decorated with punched paper leaves.

FINISHED SIZE: 4 x 5 inches (10.2 x 12.7 cm)

MATERIALS

- Template (page 123)
- Cardstock: ivory and moss green
- Pink printed paper
- Quilling paper: red and black
- Craft knife
- Ink pads: dark green, brown, and light brown
- Leaf punch
- Craft knife

QUILLING SHAPES & SCROLLS
(pages 16–18)

- Loose circle
- Half circle
- "V" scroll variation

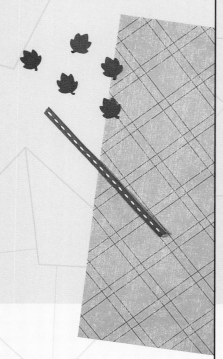

■ STEP BY STEP

1 Create a 4 x 5-inch (10.2 x 12.7 cm) card using an 8 x 5-inch (20.3 x 12.7 cm) piece of ivory cardstock.

2 Cut a piece of pink printed paper so it's slightly smaller than the card front, and adhere it to the card.

3 Cut a 1½ x 3-inch (3.8 x 7.6 cm) window in the card front. Ink the edges of the card and the window opening with light brown ink.

4 With a pencil, lightly sketch out the tree branch inside the card. Use a brown ink pad to paint the branch.

5 Punch out four leaves from moss-green cardstock. Ink the edges of the leaves with dark green ink, and adhere them to the branch.

6 For the ladybug's body, use a 1-inch (2.5 cm) strip of black quilling paper and a 10-inch (25.4 cm) length of red quilling paper. Glue them together using the end-to-end technique (see page 14). Start rolling from the black end, and then pinch the shape into a half circle.

7 Make the ladybug's head by rolling a 3-inch (7.6 cm) strip of black quilling paper into a loose circle. For the antenna, fold a 1-inch (2.5 cm) piece of black quilling paper in half, and roll a "V" scroll variation. Place the quilled shapes on the card front, and glue them in place.

Savvy Swirls

En masse, quilled "S" scrolls weave a flowing pattern that is mesmerizing to behold. The subtle color palette and accents lend this card an air of sophistication.

FINISHED SIZE: 4 x 5 inches (10.2 x 12.7 cm)

MATERIALS

- Cardstock: light blue
- Cardstock quilling paper: four shades of green
- Coordinating floral-printed paper
- Ribbon
- Tape

QUILLING SHAPES & SCROLLS
(page 18)

- "S" scroll

■ STEP BY STEP

1 Fold an 8 x 5-inch (20.3 x 12.7 cm) piece of light blue cardstock in half to create a basic folded card that measures 4 x 5 inches (10.2 x 12.7 cm).

2 Cut a rectangle from floral-printed paper, and adhere it to the card front.

3 Trim a length of ribbon, and wrap it around the card front. Tape the ends to the inside of the card.

4 With each green color, cut a 12-inch (30.5 cm) and an 8-inch (20.3 cm) cardstock quilling strip. Roll the strips into "S" scrolls.

5 Arrange the scrolls on the card from darkest to lightest, and use tweezers to glue them in place.

Variation: Need a gift tag instead? Customize it with sophisticated quilled swirls.

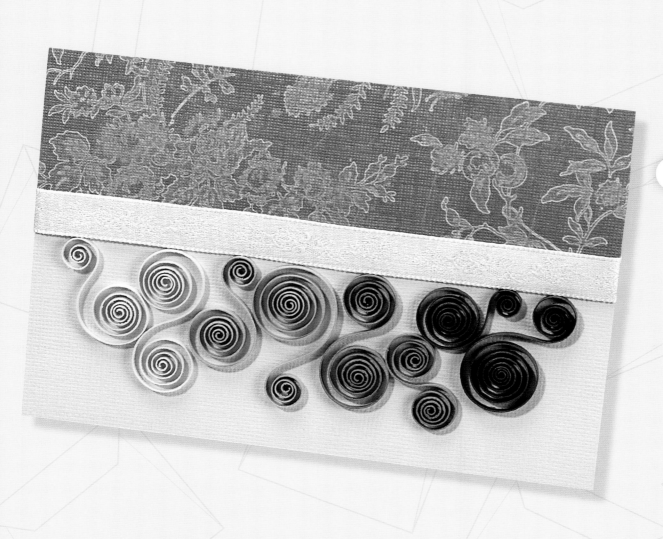

Bejeweled Crown

By combining just two quilled shapes, you can fashion a crown fit for royalty. When created in masculine colors, this design also makes a fine Father's Day card—making dad king for a day.

FINISHED SIZE: 5 x 2½ inches (12.7 x 6.4 cm)

MATERIALS

- Template (page 123)
- Cardstock: white and pink
- Pink printed paper
- Quilling paper: fuchsia
- Mini-scalloped scissors
- Rhinestone gems
- Hole punch
- Pink chiffon ribbon

QUILLING SHAPES & SCROLLS
(pages 16–17)

- Triangle
- Diamond

▶ STEP BY STEP

1 Trim a piece of pink cardstock to make a 5 x 2½-inch (12.7 x 6.4 cm) tag.

2 Cut a slightly smaller rectangle from the pink printed paper, and adhere it on top of the tag.

3 Cut a circle that measures 1¾ inches (4.4 cm) in diameter from the white cardstock. Adhere the white circle to another piece pink cardstock, and use mini-scalloped scissors to trim a pink edge around the circle. Adhere the circles to the tag.

4 For a crown, roll three 8-inch (20.3 cm) strips of fuchsia quilling paper into loose circles. Pinch two of the shapes into right-angle triangles. Pinch the center shape into a diamond. Glue the shapes in place.

5 Add rhinestones as shown.

6 Punch a hole in the top left corner of the tag, and add a length of pink ribbon.

Variation: Personalize your tag by adding someone's name or using their favorite color.

Divine Valentine

Rich red hues, swooping scrolls, and a bold heart shape create this romantic Valentine's Day card. For a different look, fill the heart with another quilled shape, or cover the whole card front with scrolls.

FINISHED SIZE: 4 x 4 inches (10.8 x 10.8 cm)

MATERIALS

- Template (page 120)
- Cardstock: crimson and pink
- Floral-print paper
- Quilling paper: crimson
- Red ink pad
- White chiffon ribbon
- Crimson acrylic paint and paintbrush

QUILLING SHAPES & SCROLLS
(page 18)

- Swooping scroll

■ STEP BY STEP

1 Fold a 4 x 8-inch (10.2 x 20.3 cm) rectangle of crimson cardstock in half to create a square 4 x 4-inch (10.2 x 10.2 cm) card.

2 Cut a square of floral-print paper slightly smaller than the card front. Rub the edges with red ink, and adhere the square to the card.

3 Attach the ribbon around the front and back of the card using glue, leaving the ends loose where the card opens.

4 Cut a 2½-inch (6.4 cm) square from pink cardstock. Rub the edges with red ink and adhere it to the card front over the ribbon. Lightly trace the shape of a heart with a pencil and then use crimson paint to trace the outline.

5 Use nine 2-inch (5 cm) strips of crimson quilling paper to roll swooping scrolls. Place the quilled shapes inside the heart shape, and glue them in place.

6 Tie the loose ribbon ends in a bow for a decorative closure.

67

Football Fanatic

Go team! You'll score big points with the recipient of this card. Customize it using his or her favorite team's colors.

FINISHED SIZE: 4½ x 3 inches (11.4 x 7.6 cm)

MATERIALS

- Template (page 124)
- Cardstock: printed blue, printed navy, and white
- Cardstock quilling paper: brown
- Quilling paper: white
- Craft knife
- Sandpaper
- Black ink pad
- Star brads
- Hole punch
- Ribbon
- Black fine-tip pen

QUILLING SHAPES & SCROLLS

(pages 16–17)
- Half circle

■ STEP BY STEP

1 Create a 4½ x 3-inch (11.4 x 7.6 cm) card by folding a 4½ x 6-inch (11.4 x 15.2 cm) piece of navy printed cardstock in half.

2 Cut the letter "B" from blue printed cardstock. Using a block computer font, print the letter to the right size, place it over the blue cardstock, and cut the letter out with a craft knife.

3 Sand the edges of the card front and the "B." Adhere the "B" to the card front.

4 Cut a triangle from white cardstock, rub the edges with black ink, and adhere it to the card front.

5 Attach two star brads to the card. Punch two holes at the corner, and attach ribbons.

6 For the football, roll two 8-inch (20.3 cm) brown cardstock quilling strips into flat half circles. Glue the two halves together. Cut a small length of white quilling paper, and draw in stitching lines with a black pen. Glue the quilled football in place on the card.

Variation: Creating a football field is easy with a quilling paper goal and yardage markers.

Crafty Cat

As any cat lover can attest, felines and yarn just naturally attract. Use your quilling shape repertoire to create this mischievous kitten and then embellish the card with texture-rich novelty yarns.

FINISHED SIZE: 4 inches (10.2 cm) in diameter

MATERIALS

- Template (page 124)
- Cardstock: purple
- Quilling paper: pink and pale pink
- Various yarns
- Tape
- Black fine-tip pen
- Wiggly eyes

QUILLING SHAPES & SCROLLS

(pages 16–18)

- Tight marquise
- Teardrop
- Half circle
- Folded loop
- Loose scroll
- Off-center circle

■ STEP BY STEP

1 Create a circular 4-inch-diameter (10.2 cm) card using purple cardstock, keeping the fold at the top. Wrap different yarns around the card front, and use transparent tape to secure it on the inside of the card. Leave an empty area on the front of the card for the quilled cat.

2 For the cat's head and face, glue a 16-inch (40.6 cm) pale pink and a 32-inch (81.2 cm) pink quilling strip together, following the end–to-end technique (page 14), to make a 48-inch (122 cm) paper strip. Starting from the pale pink end, roll it into a tight marquise. With a black pen, draw the nose, whiskers, and mouth, and glue two wiggly eyes to the face.

3 For the ears, roll two 3-inch (7.6 cm) strips of pink quilling paper into teardrops.

4 Make the cat's body by rolling a 16-inch (40.6 cm) length of pink into an off-center circle. Then pinch the shape into a long half circle.

5 For the feet, roll two 4-inch (10.2 cm) pieces of pink quilling paper into teardrops.

6 Create the legs by cutting two 2-inch (5 cm) lengths of pink quilling paper. Fold each one in half, place glue between the fold, and bend it into a small loop. Glue to the feet and body.

7 For the front paws, use a 3-inch (7.6 cm) length of pink quilling paper. Using sharp scissors, cut this paper strip in half lengthwise to make two narrow ⅟₁₆-inch-wide (1.6 mm) paper strips, and roll them into half circles.

8 For the tail, roll a 2-inch (5 cm) piece of pink quilling paper into a loose scroll. Glue all the quilled pieces in place on the card front.

71

Birthday Candles

Quilled candle flames and confetti say birthday fun is afoot. A special trick—rolling two quilling strips together—makes the candle flames really come alive.

FINISHED SIZE: 8 x 4 inches (20.3 x 10.2 cm)

MATERIALS

- Cardstock: black, white, and red
- Multicolored printed paper
- Quilling paper: red, orange, yellow, green, and blue
- Black ink pad
- "Happy Birthday" stamp
- Mini-scalloped scissors
- Foam adhesive squares

QUILLING SHAPES & SCROLLS

(pages 16–18)

- Teardrop
- Loose scroll
- "S" scroll

■ STEP BY STEP

1 Fold an 8 x 8-inch (20.3 x 20.3 cm) piece of black cardstock in half to make a card that measures 8 x 4 inches (20.3 x 10.2 cm). Trim the top and side of the card at an angle, using the photo as a guide.

2 Stamp "Happy Birthday" on a piece of white cardstock. Adhere the white piece to a section of red cardstock, and trim around the edges to create a border. Adhere both pieces to the card front.

3 Use decorative scissors to make the candlesticks using the multicolored printed paper, and adhere them to the card with foam squares.

4 For each candle flame, stack and glue the ends of two 6-inch (15.2 cm) lengths of yellow and orange quilling paper together (see rolling multiple strips on page 14). Roll the pieces at the same time into a teardrop shape, and then pinch to curve the point (page 17).

5 For the party streamers, roll short lengths of quilling paper into loose and "S" scrolls. Trim small pieces of quilling paper to create confetti. Glue the pieces in place on the card front.

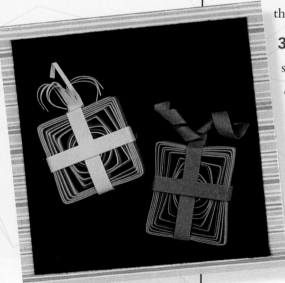

Variation: *Got some leftover paper? Try making this matching gift package card.*

Boisterous Bubbles

For a clever shortcut, use a purchased card as a base and highlight the pattern with quilled shapes. Off-center quilled circles mimic the dot pattern on this store-bought card.

FINISHED SIZE: 4 x 5 inches (10.2 x 12.7 cm)

MATERIALS & TOOLS
- Preprinted card with a circular design (or make your own)
- Quilling paper: light blue, moss green, and pink
- Brown ribbon
- Tape

QUILLING SHAPES & SCROLLS
(pages 16–17)
- Off-center circle

■ STEP BY STEP

1 Attach brown ribbon around the bottom front edge of a 4 x 5-inch (10.2 x 12.7 cm) preprinted pattern card, securing the ends with tape on the inside of the card.

2 Using the light blue, moss green, and pink quilling strips, roll off-center circles that will fit into the circles on the printed card.

3 Glue the circles to the card with the centers angled in the same direction.

Variation: Try rolling multiple papers at once or use different accents to create your own unique look.

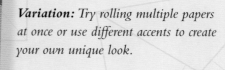

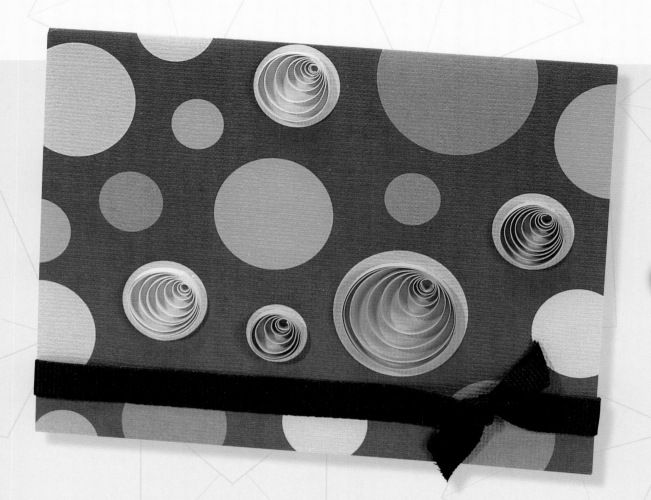

Sunrise Surprise

Good day sunshine! Quilled triangular rays radiate from a bright off-center circle while tiny pierced holes subtly frame the design.

FINISHED SIZE: 2 x 2 inches (5 x 5 cm)

MATERIALS

- Template (page 124)
- Cardstock: white
- Quilling paper: orange, deep yellow, and yellow
- Hole punch
- Ribbon

QUILLING SHAPES & SCROLLS

(pages 16–17)

- Triangle
- Off-center circle

■ STEP BY STEP

1 Fold a 4 x 2-inch (10.2 x 5 cm) piece of white cardstock in half to create a basic 2-inch-square (5 cm) card.

2 Use a needle tool to pierce holes around the card front. Punch a hole in one corner, and attach a length of ribbon to the card.

3 For the sun, roll a 16-inch (40.6 cm) strip of orange quilling paper into an off-center circle.

4 Make the sun's rays by rolling different lengths—4 to 8 inches (10.2 to 20.3 cm)—of yellow and deep yellow quilling paper into triangles. Glue each piece in place on the card front.

Variation: Catch some rays with this cheery card, complete with ribbon and an off-center circle sun.

Quilt Blocks

Quilting or quilling? Create and adapt the traditional shapes in quilting to the basic shapes in quilling. The key is to make the pieces as uniform as possible.

FINISHED SIZE: 5 x 5 inches (12.7 x 12.7 cm)

MATERIALS

- Template (page 124)
- Printed pattern paper
- Cardstock: light blue and ivory
- Quilling paper: light blue, light purple, and dark purple
- Sewing machine and thread
- Tape

QUILLING SHAPES & SCROLLS

(pages 16–17)

- Square
- Teardrop
- Rectangle
- Diamond
- Triangle

STEP BY STEP

1 Fold a 10 x 5-inch (25.4 x 12.7 cm) section of printed pattern paper in half to make a basic folded 5-inch (12.7 cm) square card.

2 Cut a 3½-inch (7.6 cm) square using light blue cardstock. Cut four small 1½-inch (3.8 cm) squares using ivory cardstock, and adhere them, in a grid, to the light blue cardstock.

3 Machine-stitch around the ivory pieces, taping the loose threads to the back of the blue piece. Adhere the square piece to the card front.

4 To make the quilt blocks, use a circle sizer to roll 8-inch (20.3 cm) lengths of different colored quilling strips into the following shapes: one square and four teardrops for the four-point star, six rectangles for the rolling star, eight right-angle triangles for the pinwheel, and eight diamonds for the eight-point star.

5 Use tweezers to glue the pieces together before gluing them in place on the ivory cardstock squares.

Variation: Use a quilled quilt design—like this eight-point star—as a focal point for a gift tag.

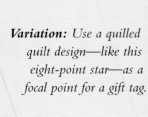

79

A+ Teacher

Give your child's favorite teacher more than just an apple. Send a sweet and thoughtful card with a quilled boy or girl to express your appreciation.

FINISHED SIZE: 4 x 4 inches (10.2 x 10.2 cm)

MATERIALS

- Template (page 121)
- Cardstock: brown, light blue, and black
- Quilling paper: red, green, pale peach, blue, black, and brown
- White crayon
- Black fine-tip pen
- Crimpter tool

QUILLING SHAPES & SCROLLS

(pages 16–17)

- Tight circle
- Teardrop with tail
- Marquise
- Square
- Rectangle

Variation: Add glitter glue, ponytails, and a cheery fringed flower to make a great gift tag for a favorite teacher.

■ STEP BY STEP

1 Fold an 8 x 4-inch (20.3 x 10.2 cm) piece of brown cardstock in half to make a 4 x 4-inch (10.2 x 10.2 cm) basic folded square card. Cut a piece of light blue cardstock that is slightly smaller than the card, and adhere it to the card front.

2 Cut a 2 x 3-inch (5 x 7.6 cm) rectangle from black cardstock, and write "thank you" on it with a white crayon. Cut a narrow brown rectangular piece, glue it to the bottom of the chalkboard, and draw a wood grain texture with a black pen.

3 For the apple, roll an 8-inch (20.3 cm) strip of red quilling paper into a square. Roll a 2-inch (5 cm) strip of green quilling paper into a marquise for the leaf.

4 For the little boy's face, roll a 36-inch (91.4 cm) piece of pale peach into a tight circle. Draw the eyes and mouth with the black pen. Crimp a length of brown quilling paper, and trim a

small piece to glue on top of his head for hair.

5 For the boy's body, roll a 12-inch (30.5 cm) length of blue quilling paper into a rectangle. For his arms and hands, roll two 2-inch (5 cm) lengths of pale peach quilling paper into teardrops with tails, and trim the arms to the appropriate length.

6 For his legs and feet, roll two 2-inch (5 cm) lengths of black quilling paper into teardrops with tails, and trim the legs to the appropriate length. Glue each piece in place on the card front.

Ruby Bloom

Simple circles of retro-patterned paper really make this quilled flower pop. For even more pizzazz, embellish the center with rhinestones.

FINISHED SIZE: 4 x 4 inches (10.2 x 10.2 cm)

MATERIALS

- Template (page 122)
- Cardstock: black and white
- Various printed papers: black, white, and red
- Cardstock quilling strips: red
- Black ink pad
- Rhinestones

QUILLING SHAPES & SCROLLS

(pages 16–17)

- Marquise

■ STEP BY STEP

1 Create a basic square 4 x 4-inch (10.2 x 10.2 cm) card using an 8 x 4-inch (20.3 x 10.2 cm) piece of white cardstock.

2 Using the printed papers, cut four circles that measure 1¾ inches (4.4 cm) in diameter, and adhere them to the card front. Color the edges of the card with black ink.

3 Create the flower petals with red cardstock quilling strips and a circle sizer. Cut eight 12-inch (30.5 cm) lengths, roll the strips into marquise shapes, and glue them together to create the flower shape.

4 For the flower's center, cut a small circle that is ¾ inch (1.9 cm) in diameter from the black cardstock. Glue the black circle on top of the flower center, and glue rhinestones on top of the circle. Place the flower on the card front, and glue it in place.

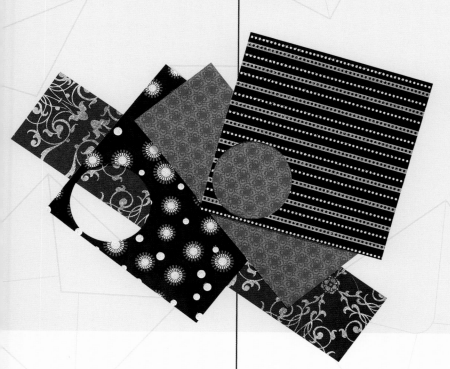

Scrolled Window

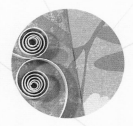

Surround a dear photo with a border of graceful scrolls. Try this simple technique on a window card or on a mat for a framed picture.

MATERIALS

- Template (page 123)
- Cardstock: ivory
- Floral and textured printed coordinating papers
- Quilling paper: ivory
- Light blue ink pad
- Craft knife

QUILLING SHAPES & SCROLLS

(page 18)
- "C" scroll
- "S" scroll
- Swooping scroll

■ STEP BY STEP

1 Fold a 5½ x 8½-inch (14 x 21.6 cm) piece of ivory cardstock in half to create a basic 5½ x 4¼-inch (14 x 10.8 cm) card.

2 Cut a 5½ x 4¼-inch (14 x 10.8 cm) rectangular piece from floral-printed paper. Adhere it to the card front, and color the edges with light blue ink.

3 Cut a 3 x 3½-inch (7.6 x 8.9 cm) rectangle from blue printed paper, rub the edges with light blue ink, and adhere it to the card.

4 Cut a window through the card front.

5 For the scrolled border, use random lengths—from 4 to 6 inches (10.2 to 15.2 cm)—of ivory quilling paper. Roll them into swooping "C" and "S" scrolls. Glue the quilled pieces in place on the card front.

Special Delivery

This is a great choice for that little boy on the go! Make this unique tag for a baby announcement or a birthday treat.

FINISHED SIZE: 4 x 4 inches (10.2 x 10.2 cm)

MATERIALS

- Template (page 121)
- Cardstock: brown and moss green
- Car-themed and light blue gingham printed paper
- Quilling paper: blue and brown
- Corner rounder punch
- Brown ink pad
- Mini-scalloped scissors
- "Special Delivery" stamp
- Alphabet letter stamps (lowercase)
- Hole punch
- Brown packaging string

QUILLING SHAPES & SCROLLS

(pages 16–17)

- Tight circle
- Square

■ STEP BY STEP

1 Cut a square 4-inch (10.2 cm) tag from brown cardstock.

2 Cut a 1½ x 3-inch (3.8 x 7.6 cm) rectangle from the gingham printed paper. Cut a 3 x 3-inch (7.6 x 7.6 cm) square from the car-themed paper. Round all of the corners, color the edges with brown ink, and adhere each piece to the tag front.

3 For the postage stamp, cut a 1 x ¾-inch (2.5 x 1.9 cm) rectangle from car-themed paper, and adhere it to the moss green cardstock. Trim around the rectangle with mini-scalloped scissors, rub the edges with brown ink, and adhere it to the tag front.

4 Stamp "Special Delivery," "to," and "from" on the tag with brown ink. Punch a hole in the corner, and attach string.

5 For the back half of the car, roll an 8-inch (20.3 cm) piece of blue quilling paper into a square. For the front half, roll a 4-inch (10.2 cm) piece of blue quilling paper into a square. Glue the two squares together.

6 Make the wheels by rolling two 4-inch (10.2 cm) lengths of brown quilling paper into tight circles. Glue the quilled pieces to the tag front.

Lazy Daisy

This card needs no occasion to be given. Brighten someone's day with a cheery quilled daisy—just because. Trimming the cardstock edges with decorative scissors gives the flower's center a ruffled look.

FINISHED SIZE: 4 x 4 inches (10.2 x 10.2 cm)

MATERIALS

- Template (page 122)
- Cardstock: white, moss green, and yellow
- Color coordinated printed paper
- Cardstock quilling strips: white
- Brown ink pad
- Hole punch
- White ribbon
- Deckle-edged scissors

QUILLING SHAPES & SCROLLS
(pages 16–17)

- Loose circle
- Teardrops

■ STEP BY STEP

1 Create a square 4 x 4-inch (10.2 x 10.2 cm) card by folding an 8 x 4-inch (20.3 x 10.2 cm) piece of white cardstock in half.

2 Using the printed paper, cut four 2 x 2-inch (5 x 5 cm) squares, and adhere them to the card front. Ink the edges of the card front with the brown ink pad.

3 Cut a circle that measures 2¼ inch (5.7 cm) in diameter from moss green cardstock, ink the edge with brown ink, and adhere it to the card, using the photo as a reference.

4 Punch two holes in the upper left corner of the card, and tie on two short strips of ribbon.

5 For the daisy petals, use a circle sizer to roll eight 12-inch (30.5 cm) strips of white cardstock quilling paper into teardrops, and glue them together to create the flower shape.

6 For the center of daisy, use the deckle-edged scissors to trim a ⅛-inch (3 mm) quilling strip using yellow cardstock. Cut one 6-inch (15.2 cm) strip, and roll it into a loose circle. Ink the edges, and glue it on top of the daisy. Place the quilled daisy on the card front, and glue it in place.

Pinwheel Blossoms

The combination of red patterned papers, stitching, and beautiful scrolled flowers turn this card into a definite keeper, but you'll enjoy giving it away.

MATERIALS

- Template (page 122)
- Cardstock: red
- Various red printed papers
- Quilling paper: white and moss green
- Red ink pad
- Sewing machine
- White thread
- Tape

QUILLING SHAPES & SCROLLS

(pages 16–18)

- Loose circle
- Teardrop
- Scrolled flower
- Swooping scroll

■ STEP BY STEP

1 Fold a 7-inch (17.8 cm) square of red cardstock in half to create a 7 x 3½-inch (17.8 x 8.9 cm) card.

2 Cut four rectangular pieces of red printed paper to cover the card front. Attach the pieces to the card front and ink the edges with red ink.

3 Machine-stitch along the top and sides of the card front, using tape to secure the loose threads on the inside.

4 To make the large flower, glue four 4-inch (10.2 cm) lengths of white quilling paper together into a scrolled flower shape, and roll each end in toward the center. For the flower center, roll an 8-inch (20.3 cm) length of white quilling paper into a loose circle.

5 For the smaller flower, glue four 2-inch (5 cm) lengths of white quilling paper into a scrolled flower shape, rolling each end in toward the center. For the flower center, roll a 4-inch (10.2 cm) length of quilling paper into a loose circle.

6 Roll three 4-inch (10.2 cm) lengths of moss-green quilling paper into swooping scrolls to make the stems.

7 For the leaves, roll three 8-inch (20.3 cm) lengths of moss-green quilling paper into curved teardrops. Place the quilled shapes on the card front, and glue them in place.

90

Goldfish Bowl

With no daily feedings needed and no fishbowl to clean, this fanciful goldfish in its bowl-shaped card could very well be the perfect pet. Have a crimper on hand to shape your cardstock pieces and quilling strips.

FINISHED SIZE: 4 x 5 inches (10.2 x 12.7 cm)

MATERIALS
- Template (page 124)
- Cardstock: white and blue
- Water-pattern printed paper
- Quilling paper: yellow and deep yellow
- Crimper tool
- Foam adhesives squares
- Blue ink pad
- Wiggly eye
- Hole punch (two sizes)

QUILLING SHAPES & SCROLLS
(pages 16–17)
- Half circle
- Tight circle
- Off-center circle

STEP BY STEP

1 Create a basic 4 x 5-inch (10.2 x 12.7 cm) folded card from an 8 x 5-inch (20.3 x 12.7 cm) piece of white cardstock, making sure the fold is at the top, long edge.

2 Cut a 5-inch-diameter (12.7 cm) circle from blue cardstock. Create a frame for the fish by cutting a small circle out of the blue cardstock off to one side, using the photo as a guide. Run the blue circle through the crimper, keeping the crimp direction in mind when inserting your piece.

3 With scissors, trim a straight edge along the crimped piece to create the top of the water. Place the blue crimped piece over the card front, and trim the bowl shape with scissors.

4 Cut a circle from the water-pattern paper that is slightly larger than the circle cutout in the blue crimped piece.

5 Glue the circle to the card front. Adhere the blue crimped piece using foam adhesive so the water-pattern circle shows through the circle cutout, and color the edges with blue ink.

6 For the fish's body, roll a 16-inch (40.6 cm) strip of yellow quilling paper into an off-center circle, and pinch the end to create a teardrop shape. For the fish's tail, roll a 12-inch (30.5 cm) length of deep yellow quilling paper into a half circle.

7 Roll two 2-inch (5 cm) pieces of yellow quilling paper into tight circles for the lips. For the fish's fins, crimp a strip of deep yellow quilling paper and cut them into small pieces.

8 Glue the goldfish pieces in place on the water-patterned paper, and glue on a wiggly eye. Punch a few circles from the white cardstock, and attach them for bubbles.

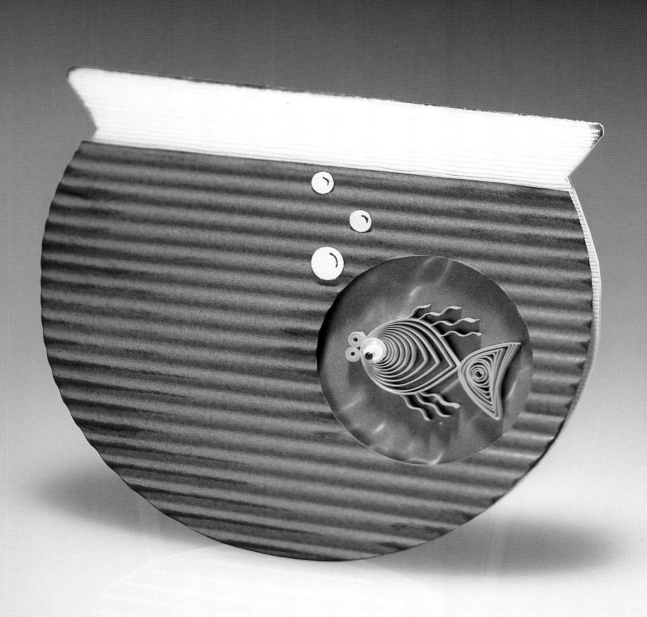

Angel Trio

Spread joy and peace with a choir of quilled angels on your holiday greeting cards. The off-center circle technique creates the wonderful effect on the angels' flowing robes.

FINISHED SIZE: 4 x 8 inches (10.2 x 20.3 cm)

MATERIALS

- Template (page 121)
- Cardstock: crimson
- Green printed paper in two different patterns
- Quilling paper: white, pale peach, and yellow
- Crimson ribbon

QUILLING SHAPES & SCROLLS

(pages 16–17)

- Tight circle
- Marquise
- Off-center circle

■ STEP BY STEP

1 Fold an 8 x 8-inch (20.3 x 20.3 cm) piece of crimson cardstock in half to make a 4 x 8-inch (10.2 x 20.3 cm) card.

2 Cut a piece of green swirling paper that is smaller than the card front, and adhere it to the card. Cut a piece of striped paper that is approximately half as tall as the card front, tear the top edge, and adhere the piece to the bottom of the card front.

3 Cut three crimson cardstock circles that measure 2 inches (5 cm) in diameter, and adhere them to the card. Tie three ribbons into bows, and attach one at the top of each circle.

4 For each quilled angel's head, roll a 16-inch (40.6 cm) length of pale peach quilling paper into a tight circle.

5 For each angel's body, roll a 16-inch (40.6 cm) strip of white quilling paper into a loose circle. Make the loose circle into an off-center circle, and then pinch it into a triangle shape.

6 Make the wings by rolling two 8-inch (20.3 cm) pieces of white quilling paper into marquise shapes and pinching the ends to make them curve (page 17).

7 To make the halo, use a small strip of yellow quilling paper, and glue the ends to create an oval loop. Using the photo as a guide, place the quilled shapes on the card front, and glue them in place.

Soccer Star

Score! Your favorite soccer lover will appreciate this sport-themed card. Try sanding printed cardstock to give your card a worn and rugged look.

FINISHED SIZE: 4 x 5 inches (10.2 x 12.7 cm)

MATERIALS & TOOLS

- Template (page 124)
- Cardstock: printed brown, printed green, and black
- Cardstock quilling strips: black and white
- Sandpaper
- Adhesive mesh
- Ribbon
- Star brads
- Rub-on letters

QUILLING SHAPES & SCROLLS
(pages 16–17)

- Loose circle
- Marquise

■ STEP BY STEP

1 Create a basic folded 4 x 5-inch (10.2 x 12.7 cm) card using an 8 x 5-inch (20.3 x 12.7 cm) section of brown printed cardstock, and sand the edges.

2 Cut a 2-inch (5 cm) square piece of black cardstock. Cut a 2-inch (5 cm) square piece of green cardstock, sand the edges, and adhere it to the black piece.

3 Using the photo as a guide, cut a piece of adhesive mesh and adhere it to the card front, followed by the black and green squares.

4 Trim a length of ribbon to fit the card front. Attach it to the card with star brads, and use rub-on letters to create "Super Star" on the ribbon.

5 Create the soccer ball using black and white cardstock quilling strips. Roll six 6-inch (15.2 cm) lengths of white quilling strips and one 6-inch (15.2 cm) piece of black into loose circles. Roll six 3-inch (7.6 cm) lengths of black quilling strips into marquise shapes. Glue the loose circles and marquise shapes together, using the photo as a guide. Use tweezers to help hold and glue the quilled pieces together.

6 Use a black quilling strip to glue around the quilled pieces, and glue the soccer ball to the card front.

Petal Power

Use a variety of basic quilled shapes to produce a handsome bouquet of flowers. The fun floral print and narrow fabric ribbon tie all the elements together.

FINISHED SIZE: 5 x 4 inches (12.7 x 10.2 cm)

MATERIALS

- Cardstock: light green
- Floral-printed paper
- Quilling paper: coordinating colors
- Ribbon
- Colored brads

QUILLING SHAPES & SCROLLS

(pages 16–17)

- Loose circle
- Teardrop
- Marquise
- Triangle
- Half circle

■ STEP BY STEP

1 Create a basic folded 5 x 4–inch (12.7 x 10.2 cm) card using an 5 x 8–inch (12.7 x 20.3 cm) piece of light green cardstock.

2 Cut a 5 x 2-inch (12.7 x 5 cm) rectangle from floral-printed paper, and adhere it to the card front. Glue a thin strip of ribbon across the face of the card.

3 For each flower, roll five 4-inch (10.2 cm) lengths of quilling paper into different petal shapes—loose circles, triangles, teardrops, marquise, and half circles.

4 Insert colored brads to create each flower center. Place the quilled shapes on the card front, and glue them in place.

99

Garden Party

You don't need a green thumb to create this gardening-themed tag. Attach it to a plant, a flowerpot, or a new set of gardening tools.

FINISHED SIZE: 5 x 2½ inches (12.7 x 6.4 cm)

MATERIALS

- Template (page 122)
- Cardstock: dark purple and moss green
- Green leaf printed paper
- Quilling paper: gray, purple, pink, gold, and forest green
- Black fine-tip pen
- Embroidery thread and needle
- Hole punch
- Purple ribbon

QUILLING SHAPES & SCROLLS

(pages 16–17)

- Teardrop
- Triangle
- Square
- Half circle
- Marquise

■ STEP BY STEP

1 Create a 5 x 2½-inch (12.7 x 6.4 cm) tag using dark purple cardstock. Cut a slightly smaller rectangle from printed leaf paper, and adhere it to the front of the tag. Add the text "to" and "from" with the black pen.

2 Cut a 2½ x 2½-inch (6.4 x 6.4 cm) square from moss-green cardstock, and adhere it to the tag, using the picture as a guide. Use embroidery thread and a needle to add decorative stitches to each corner.

3 For the quilled garden tool handles, roll two 8-inch (20.3 cm) strips of purple quilling paper into narrow teardrops.

4 Make the fork using a 1-inch (2.5 cm) length of gray quilling paper, and fold it in half. Place glue near the fold, press together, and fold the ends into an "M" shape. Trim the ends. For the trowel, roll an 8-inch (20.3 cm) strip of gray quilling paper into a triangle.

5 Roll an 8-inch (20.3 cm) length of gold quilling paper into a square to make the flowerpot. Pinch and curve two of the points to make the rim of the flowerpot (page 17).

6 For the flower, roll an 8-inch (20.3 cm) piece of pink quilling paper into a half circle, and curve the points. Create the leaves by rolling two 4-inch (10.2 cm) lengths of forest-green quilling paper into curved marquise shapes (see page 17). Glue the shapes in place.

7 Punch a hole in the top of the tag. Thread the ribbon through the hole, and tie a bow.

to:

from:

Mini Kisses

Who can resist this totally kissable mini card? Embellished with heart-shaped brads and quilled shapes, it's sure to make your special someone feel, well, special.

FINISHED SIZE: 2 x 2 inches (5.1 x 5.1 cm)

MATERIALS
- Template (page 120)
- Cardstock: red
- Vellum heart paper
- Quilling paper: red
- Alphabet stickers
- Heart brads

QUILLING SHAPES & SCROLLS
(pages 16–17)
- Teardrop
- Half circle

■ STEP BY STEP

1 Fold a 4 x 2-inch (10.2 x 5 cm) rectangle of red cardstock in half to create a 2 x 2-inch (5 x 5 cm) card. Adhere "X" and "O"-shaped stickers on the card front.

2 Cut a square of vellum that is slightly smaller than the card front. Attach the vellum to the card with brads.

3 For the top lip, roll two 8-inch (20.3 cm) strips of red quilling paper into teardrops.

4 For the bottom lip, roll a 16-inch (40.6 cm) length of red quilling paper into an elongated half circle shape. Place the quilled shapes on the vellum, and glue them in place.

Variation: *A ribbon-hinged circular card makes the perfect canvas for your lips. Or skip the lips altogether and use the two quilled teardrops to make cute mini hearts.*

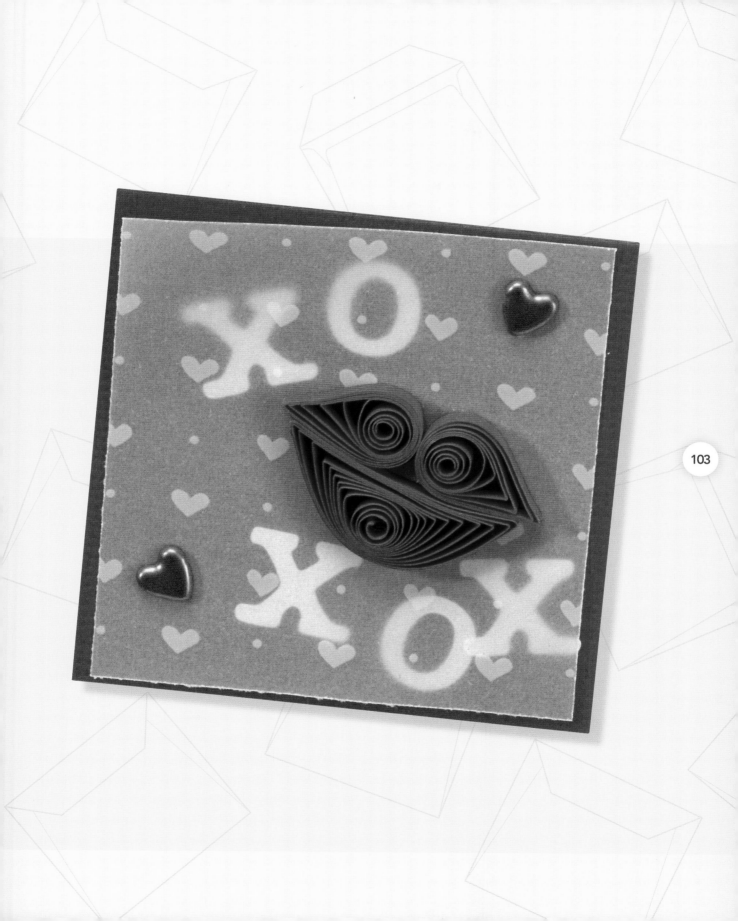

Perfect Pumpkin

Fall is the time to place a plump pumpkin on the front porch. This year, use cardstock quilling strips to create the perfect pumpkin, just right for a hearty seasonal greeting.

FINISHED SIZE: 4 x 4 inches (10.2 x 10.2 cm)

MATERIALS

- Template (page 121)
- Cardstock: brown and orange
- Foliage and striped printed paper
- Green vellum
- Cardstock quilling strips: orange
- Quilling paper: brown and forest green
- Deckle-edged scissors
- Brads

QUILLING SHAPES & SCROLLS

(pages 16–17)

- Marquise
- Half circle
- Tight circle

■ STEP BY STEP

1 Fold a 4 x 8-inch (10.2 x 20.3 cm) piece of brown cardstock in half to create a basic square card.

2 Cut a piece of striped paper that is slightly smaller than the card front, trim the top and bottom edge with deckle-edged scissors, and adhere it to the card front.

3 Cut a 1½ x 4-inch (3.8 x 10.2 cm) piece of both the orange cardstock and foliage printed paper, trim the bottom edges with deckle-edged scissors, and adhere both pieces to the card front, with the foliage paper on top.

4 Cut a 2-inch (5 cm) square from vellum, trim the bottom side with deckle-edged scissors, and attach it to the card with two brads.

5 For the pumpkin, roll a 5-inch (12.7 cm) piece of orange cardstock quillling paper into a marquise shape. Roll two 10-inch (25.4 cm) orange quilling strips into half circles, making sure the straight edge of each half circle is the same length as the marquise. Glue the pieces together.

6 For the stem, roll a ½-inch-long (1.3 cm) brown quilling strip into a tight circle.

7 For the twisted stem, cut and twist a narrow 1-inch (2.5 cm) length of forest-green quilling paper. Place the quilled pieces on the card front, and glue them in place.

Father's Day Surprise

If your dad's got more than enough of the real thing, give him a quilled tie on Father's Day. Pick patterned accent papers to show off your dad's unique personality.

FINISHED SIZE: 4 x 4 inches (10.2 x 10.2 cm)

MATERIALS

- Template (page 120)
- Cardstock: white and brown
- Various printed papers
- Quilling paper: blue
- Blue ink pad
- Blue brads

QUILLING SHAPES & SCROLLS

(pages 16–17)

- Triangle
- Marquise

▪ STEP BY STEP

1 Fold an 8 x 4-inch (20.3 x 10.2 cm) piece of white cardstock in half to create a square 4 x 4-inch (10.2 x 10.2 cm) card.

2 Cut four 2-inch (5 cm) squares using the different printed papers, and adhere each piece to the card front. Rub each edge of the card front with blue ink.

3 Cut a circle from brown cardstock, color the edge with blue ink, and glue the circle to the card front.

4 Trace and cut out the shirt pattern using white cardstock, and adhere the shirt to the circle.

5 For the tie's knot, roll a 4-inch (10.2 cm) length of blue quilling paper into a triangle. For the tie, roll a 12-inch (30.5 cm) strip of blue quilling paper into a marquise. Place the quilled shapes on the card front, and glue them in place.

6 For extra dimension, add three blue brads along the lower left edge of the card.

Variation: Is your dad more of a red person? Mix it up with this warmer-toned Father's Day greeting.

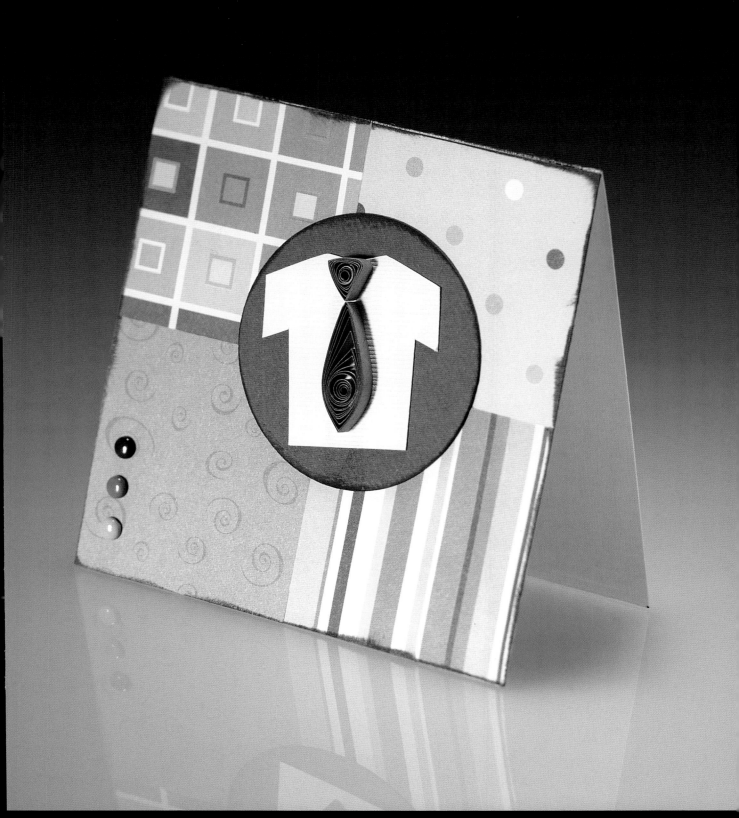

Cheers

Toast the occasion with a little bubbly and some quilled champagne glasses. Festive touches, including a shimmering gauze bow and vellum attached with silver brads, make this an ideal wedding or anniversary card.

FINISHED SIZE: 4 x 5 inches (10.2 x 12.7 cm)

MATERIALS & TOOLS

- Template (page 121)
- Cardstock: black
- Vellum
- Quilling paper: ivory
- Brads
- Rub-on letters
- Ribbon

QUILLING SHAPES & SCROLLS

(pages 16–18)

- Loose scroll
- Marquise
- Triangle

■ STEP BY STEP

1 Create a basic folded 4 x 5-inch (10.2 x 12.7 cm) card using a 4 x 10-inch (10.2 x 25.4 cm) section of black cardstock. Cut a piece of vellum that is smaller than the card front, and adhere it with two brads.

2 Rub the word "cheers" on the bottom corner of the vellum. Cut a slit in the card's fold, insert the ribbon, and tie a bow around the card front.

3 Cut a square from black cardstock, and adhere it to the card.

4 For the glass bases, roll two 3-inch (7.6 cm) pieces of ivory quilling paper into marquise shapes. For the tops, roll two 12-inch (30.5 cm) lengths of ivory quilling paper into long triangles.

5 For the glass stems, glue two ½-inch (1.3 cm) lengths of ivory quilling paper together at the middle, leaving the ends unglued. Glue the bottom and top pieces to the stem.

6 Roll three 1-inch (2.5 cm) strips of ivory quilling paper into loose scrolls to make the bubbles. Glue the quilled pieces in place on the card front, using the photo as a guide.

Ornament Tags

These one-of-a-kind ornament tags are equally suited for the holiday tree as for your gift packages. String a group of ornaments to make a unique decorative garland.

FINISHED SIZE: 2 to 2½ inches (5 to 6.4 cm) in diameter

MATERIALS
- Template (page 121)
- Red printed paper
- Holiday printed paper
- Cardstock: white and blue
- Quilling paper: crimson, green, and white
- Crimper
- Mini-scalloped scissors
- Hole punch
- Silver embroidery thread
- Silver or iridescent watercolor paint

QUILLING SHAPES & SCROLLS
(pages 16–18)
- Loose circle
- Marquise
- Heart scroll

■ STEP BY STEP

RED POLKA DOT TAG

1 Create a folded 2½-inch (6.4 cm) circular tag using red printed paper, keeping the fold at the top.

2 Cut a circular piece from holiday printed paper. Cut it in half, and adhere it to the tag.

3 Cut a small rectangular piece from white cardstock, and run it through the crimper. Trim it to fit across the fold. Cut one edge with the mini-scalloped scissors, punch a hole, and adhere it to the tag.

4 To decorate the ornament with quilling, roll 4- to 8-inch (10.2 to 20.3 cm) lengths of crimson and green quilling paper into loose circles. Glue each piece in place on the tag front, and tie on a strand of silver thread.

BLUE SNOWFLAKE TAG

1 Create a folded 2-inch (5 cm) circular tag using blue cardstock, making sure the fold is at the top.

2 Cut a small rectangular piece from white cardstock, and run it through the crimper. Trim it to fit across the fold. Cut one edge with the mini-scalloped scissors, punch a hole, and adhere it to the tag.

Variation: *Try these fun ornament designs or create your own.*

110

3 For the snowflake, roll six 4-inch (10.2 cm) lengths of white quilling paper into marquise shapes, and glue them together. Roll six 2-inch (5 cm) lengths of white quilling paper into heart scrolls. Glue the heart scrolls to the marquise shapes.

4 Glue the snowflake in place on the tag, and string silver thread through the hole in the top.

5 Use the silver or iridescent watercolor paint on the top edges of the quilled snowflake and tag.

Brand New Bag

A gal can never have too many purses, so give a girlfriend this fashion-forward card. The handbag is accessorized with a ribbon handle and a two-toned quilled flower. A fancy paper clip serves as the purse's clasp.

FINISHED SIZE: 3¼ x 5 inches (8.3 x 12.7 cm)

MATERIALS

- Template (page 125)
- Cardstock: floral pattern, pink, and brown
- Quilling paper: pink and yellow
- Brown ink pad
- Brown ribbon
- Brads
- Rhinestone
- Decorative paper clip

QUILLING SHAPES & SCROLLS
(pages 16–17)

- Marquise

■ STEP BY STEP

1 Create a folded purse card (*see template*) using the floral-pattern cardstock, keeping the fold at the bottom of the card.

2 Cut a rectangular piece from the pink cardstock, and adhere it to the card front, trimming the ends flush with the card. Color the edges with brown ink.

3 Trim a length of brown ribbon, and attach it over the pink cardstock. Cut another length of ribbon, and attach it to the card front with brads for the purse's handle.

4 Cut a circle shape from the brown cardstock, and adhere it to the card front.

5 For the flower, cut six 4-inch (10.2 cm) lengths of pink and six 4-inch (10.2 cm) lengths of yellow quilling papers. Glue the pink and yellow strips together using the end-to-end technique (see page 14) so that you have six 8-inch (20.3 cm) pieces.

6 Starting at the yellow ends, roll each 8-inch (20.3 cm) strip into a marquise petal. Glue the petals together, and then glue the flower onto the brown circle.

7 Add a rhinestone to the center of the flower. Use a decorative paper clip to hold the card closed.

Variation: Need a different color for a special occasion? Try using ivory tones and fringed flowers for added elegance.

113

Autumn Leaf

There's a nip in the air and the trees are beginning to change colors. Celebrate fall with this unique tri-fold design, which includes a circular window and matching raffia.

FINISHED SIZE: 4 x 5 inches (10.2 x 12.7 cm)

MATERIALS

- Template (page 121)
- Cardstock: moss green and dark green
- Quilling paper: red, orange, and gold
- Deckle-edged scissors
- Craft knife
- Dark green ink pad
- Raffia

QUILLING SHAPES & SCROLLS
(pages 16–18)

- Marquise
- Loose scroll

▐ STEP BY STEP

1 Fold a 4 x 9-inch (10.2 x 22.9 cm) piece of moss–green cardstock twice into a 4 x 5-inch (10.2 x 12.7 cm) tri-fold card.

2 Trim the top and bottom edges with the deckle-edged scissors. Cut an oval in the upper left flap, and color the edges with green ink.

3 Cut a rectangle from the dark green cardstock so it's a little smaller than the card front, and adhere it to the inside center of the card.

4 For the leaf, roll an 8-inch (20.3 cm) strip of each color—red, orange, and gold—into a marquise, and then pinch to curve the points (page 17).

5 Roll a 1-inch (2.5 cm) length of red into a scroll for the stem. Place the quilled shapes on the card, and glue them in place.

6 Tie the raffia in a bow around the card to keep it closed.

Mini Baby Carriage

Get ooohs and aaahhs at the next baby shower with this adorable handmade card, just right for a new arrival. The peekaboo quilled baby in a carriage with button wheels will delight the new parents.

FINISHED SIZE: 2 x 2 inches (5.1 x 5.1 cm)

MATERIALS

- Template (page 121)
- Cardstock: pastel yellow
- Gingham printed paper
- Quilling paper: pastel green, white, peach, and brown or yellow (hair color)
- Hole punch
- Ribbon
- Fine-tip black pen
- Buttons

QUILLING SHAPES & SCROLLS
(pages 16–18)

- Triangle
- Loose scroll
- Tight circle

■ STEP BY STEP

1 Fold a 4 x 2-inch (10.2 x 5 cm) piece of yellow cardstock in half to create a basic square 2-inch (5 cm) card.

2 Cut a square of printed gingham that is slightly smaller than the card front, and adhere it to the card.

3 At the top left of the card, punch a hole and attach a ribbon.

4 For the baby carriage, roll a 16-inch (40.6 cm) length of green quilling paper into a large triangle. Roll three 6-inch (15.2 cm) strips into small long triangles, and glue them together. Roll a short 1-inch (2.5 cm) length of white quilling paper into a loose scroll for the handle.

5 Create the baby's face by rolling a 16-inch (40.6 cm) piece of peach quilling paper into a tight circle. Roll a short ½-inch (1.3 cm) piece of yellow or brown quilling paper into a loose scroll for the baby's hair. Use a black pen to draw the eyes and mouth. Glue each quilled shape in place on the front of the card.

6 Adhere the buttons for the carriage's wheels.

Variation: Add baby's weight and length to make a clever birth announcement.

Monogram Glam

The common tag gets an elegant update with a quilled monogram. Letters are easy to create with basic scroll shapes.

FINISHED SIZE: 2¾ x 3½ inches (7 x 8.9 cm)

MATERIALS
- Template (page 126)
- Cardstock: three shades of brown
- Cardstock quilling paper: ivory
- Hole punch
- Ribbon

QUILLING SHAPES & SCROLLS
(page 18)
- Scroll

■ STEP BY STEP

1 Create a basic oval tag with the three different shades of brown cardstock. Stack the layers, using the photo as a guide, and adhere them together.

2 Punch a hole in the tag, and attach the ribbon.

3 Make the alphabet letters starting with 2-inch (5 cm) strips of ivory cardstock quilling paper. Roll the strips into scrolls to shape each letter, using shorter or longer strips as necessary.

4 Use tweezers to help hold and glue the quilled pieces to the tag.

Variation: A monogram is a great way to personalize a card for its recipient.

NOTE
The quilled alphabet letters can be made with quilling paper or cardstock quilling strips.

Templates (actual size)

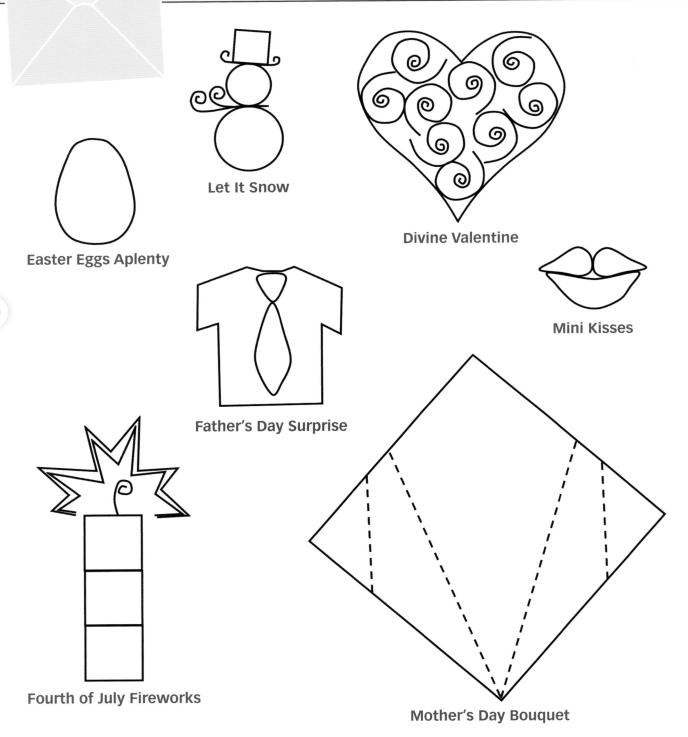

Easter Eggs Aplenty

Let It Snow

Divine Valentine

Mini Kisses

Father's Day Surprise

Fourth of July Fireworks

Mother's Day Bouquet

Autumn Leaf

Perfect Pumpkin

Angel Trio

Ornament Tags

Baby Bundle

Special Delivery

Mini Baby Carriage

Hoppy Birthday

Love Doves

A+ Teacher

Cheers

Garden Party

Lazy Daisy

Ruby Bloom

Plum Vines

122

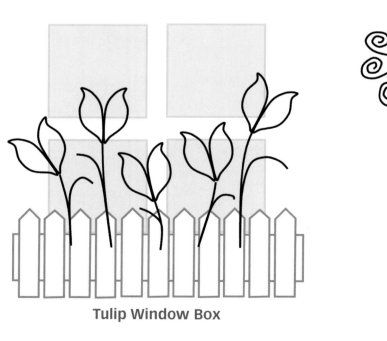

Tulip Window Box

Pinwheel Blossoms

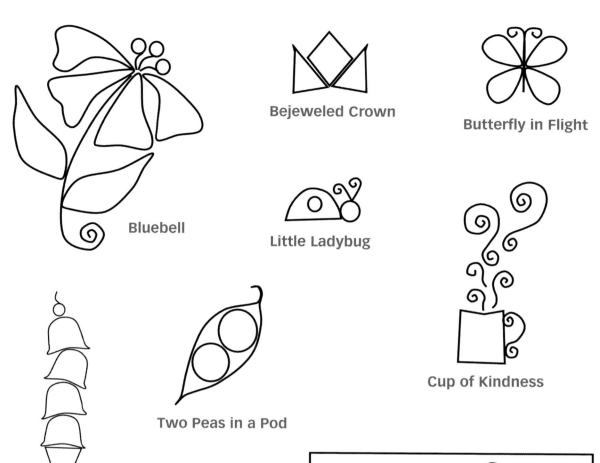

Bejeweled Crown

Butterfly in Flight

Bluebell

Little Ladybug

Cup of Kindness

Ice Cream Invite

Two Peas in a Pod

Bonbon Beauties

Scrolled Window

Soccer Star

Football Fanatic

Goldfish Bowl

Set Sail

124

Quilt Blocks

Sunrise Surprise

Sweet Treat

Crafty Cat

Cherish

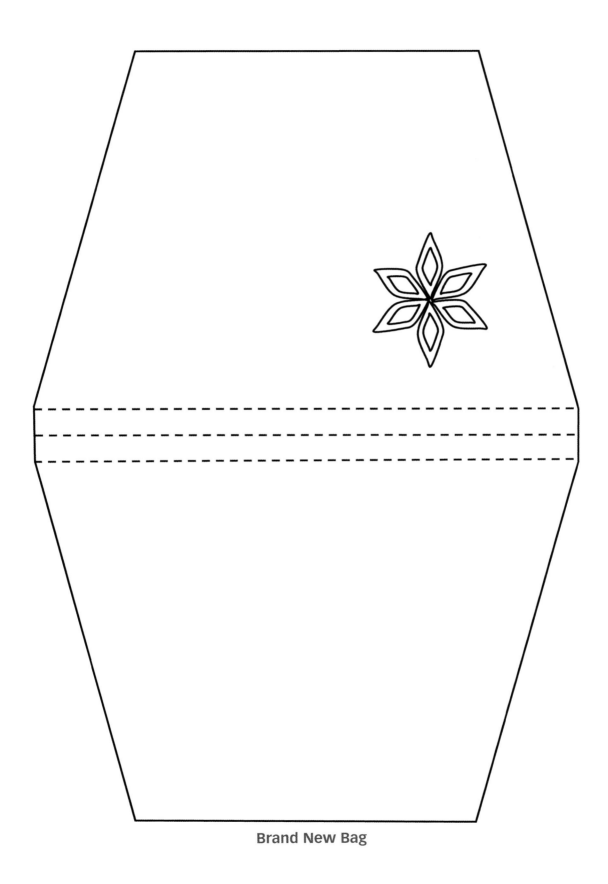

Brand New Bag

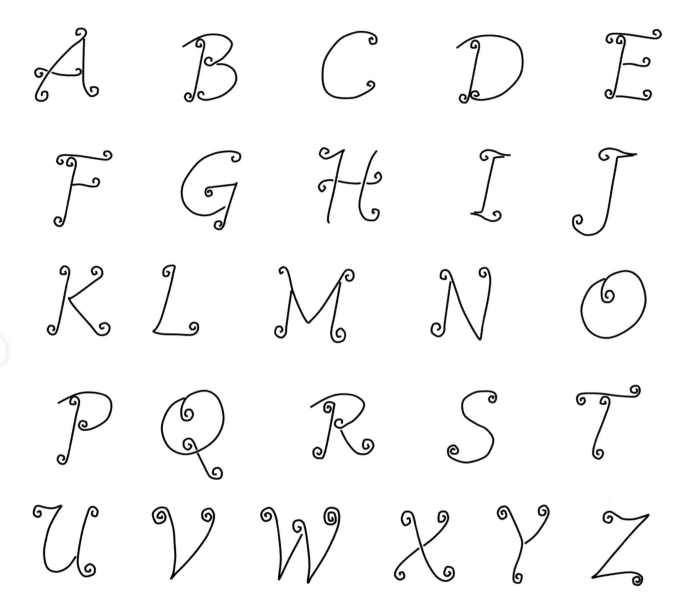

Monogram Glam

About the Author

Allison (Alli) Bartkowski started creating quilled accents for her scrapbooks and cards. From these early designs, her own line of quilling kits was born. Alli's online company—Quilled Creations, Inc. (www.quilledcreations.com)—now sells innovative quilling tools, kits, and papers. Her first book, *Paper Quilling: For the First Time*, includes step-by-step pictures to show the most popular quilling techniques. A member of the North American Quilling Guild as well as the Craft and Hobby Association, Alli loves to teach and demonstrate quilling for people of all ages at local schools and international tradeshows alike.

Acknowledgments

Thank you to Sterling Publishing and Lark Books for the wonderful opportunity to stretch my creativity with quilling again. To Terry Taylor, my editor, for your insightful ideas, guidance, and many "a-ha" moments.

Thanks to my family and friends who supported me through another book! To my husband, Dave, thank you for taking care of the house and family when I was on a "creative" roll. I am so grateful for your love and patience. To my seven-year-old daughter, Rachel, it's amazing to watch you write and illustrate your own books. You are a creative inspiration to me and everyone around you. To my five-year-old daughter, Kayla, I love how you can always make me smile. Thank you for understanding when I couldn't play chase and for your willingness to spend time quilling with me. To my parents, thank you for all of your help with the girls and the wonderful home-cooked meals. It's a blessing to have you close by. Thank you to my aunt, Una, for being my biggest cheerleader. To Tina, for always giving me words of encouragement. To my sister, Aimee, who always knows when I need a phone call or a listening ear. Finally, my deepest gratitude goes to God, for all the challenges and blessings while working on this project. I am thankful for the talents He has given to me and for His overflowing grace and peace.

Index